# MADE IN BRITAIN

**Simon Buckby** is the Campaign Director of 'Britain in Europe', a
historic coalition of patriotic pro-Europeans launched in the autumn of
1999 by Tony Blair, Gordon Brown, Kenneth Clarke, Michael Heseltine
and Charles Kennedy.
He managed the Labour Party's advertising strategy for the 1997 general
election campaign, having previously worked for John Prescott MP. He
has been a producer for LWT, a reporter for the BBC and a journalist for
*The Financial Times*.
Now aged 35, he was born and raised near Corby, an island of Scots at
the heart of Middle England, and is proud to be British.

Simon Buckby

# MADE IN BRITAIN

## The Patriotic Case for Europe and the Euro

P

PROFILE BOOKS

First published in Great Britain in 2001 by
Profile Books Ltd
58A Hatton Garden
London ECIN 8LX
www.profilebooks.co.uk

Typeset in Bembo by MacGuru
info@macguru.org.uk

Printed and bound in Great Britain by
Bookmarque Ltd, Croydon, Surrey

A CIP catalogue record for this book is available from the
British Library.

ISBN 1 86197 359 4

# Contents

For my father, of course

'And one should bear in mind that there is nothing more difficult to execute, nor more dubious of success, nor more dangerous to administer than to introduce a new order of things; for he who introduces it has all those who profit from the old order as his enemies, and he has only lukewarm allies in all those who might profit from the new.'

Niccolò Machiavelli, *The Prince*, 1532

# MADE IN BRITAIN

# Britain's National Identity

### Identity crisis?

What does it mean to be British these days? The answer used to be so obvious that the question was hardly ever asked. Britons were plainly proud of the planet's oldest democracy, which had launched the first Industrial Revolution, built the largest Empire and won two world wars. Britons were clearly a privileged people with no need for insecure introspection. But something has changed. Nowadays public debate is littered with worries about how we lost our way and who we have become. The underlying assumption is that Britain faces an identity crisis.

The turmoil is reflected in a loss of confidence in many long-standing institutions that have helped shape our Britishness. Trust in those that we elect to the Mother of Parliaments has evidently withered and the Government's greatest enemies at the last general election were apathy and cynicism. Faith in the rule of law has slumped: the criminal

justice system has been sullied by a spree of wrongful con-
victions and the Metropolitan Police Force stands officially
accused of institutionalised racism. Enthusiasm for the royal
family collapsed along with the marriage of Prince Charles
and Lady Diana Spencer. The model nuclear family has
imploded since the 1960s: in just one generation the number
of weddings has halved, the number of divorces has trebled
and the proportion of children born outside marriage has
quadrupled. In that time devotion to formal Christian wor-
ship has waned as the aggregate membership of British
churches has dropped by 40 per cent and the established
Anglican Church has lost more than a million regular adher-
ents, leaving it with half a million fewer disciples than the
Catholic Church.

Trade union membership has fallen more or less continu-
ously since 1980, slipping by 50 per cent to below eight million. Public perceptions of our Welfare State and our
National Health Service as the best in the world have given
way to the commonly held view that they are among the
worst in Europe. Ancient voluntary societies from the Boy
Scouts to the Women's Institute, the glue of social cohesion,
have suffered a slide in membership. The BBC is no longer
the voice of the nation, as Reithian values appear to have
been swept aside by cutbacks and commercialism. Our
newspapers, which reflect the country's idea of itself, have
been widely accused of sensationalism, dumbing-down and
abandoning reliable reporting in favour of sexual titillation,
cultivating celebrity and invading privacy.

Many businesses formerly resonant with Britishness have
stopped representing our national identity. Of the forty-two
notable privatisations carried out under Margaret Thatcher
and John Major, fourteen were of companies with 'British'

and four with 'National' in the title, and many have since
been re-branded. The former workshop of the world has sold
renowned names like Bentley, Jaguar, Land Rover and Rolls-
Royce, and is no longer a leader in traditional industries like
coal mining, steelworking or shipbuilding, upon which our
strength was formerly founded. Quintessential retailers such
as Marks & Spencer have struggled against competition from
abroad, and even Harrods is run by a man who cannot obtain
a British passport. The City of London is dominated by
foreign-owned institutions and its reputation as a place
where 'my word is my bond' has been dented by a series of
scandals from the Maxwell pensioners to the Lloyds' names.

This lack of enthusiasm for our emblematic institutions is
matched by a confusion in our culture. Britain is the only
country in the world where we buy our petrol in litres but
measure the performance of our vehicles in miles per gallon.
Curry has officially overtaken fish and chips as the most popular takeaway, and bars serving imported wine or bottled
lager are as common as pubs pouring authentic pints of mild
and bitter. Our television has been invaded by sitcoms about
places in the United States that most Britons have never visited, and the highest-rated portraits of home are period
dramas that romanticise the halcyon days of a bygone age.

Speakers of the Queen's English are fighting a losing battle
against American and Estuarial versions, and our professional
cricketers, footballers, rugby and tennis players – in the games
we taught the world – have been losing against almost everyone in recent years. When the Football Association turned to a
Swede to coach the England team our angst reached a crunch
point. Supporters are still wrestling with a question that cuts to
the heart of our flag-waving patriotism: do we want to retain
our native purity and lose, or try to win with foreign help?

Britain is a country in rapid transition where many of the icons of our identity are no longer secure. That is why there is a far-reaching debate about what it means to be British these days. Some have been scouring the past for the alchemy of our uniqueness while others have turned for inspiration to the civic pride of the United States or looked for our common European heritage. One recent report claimed that contemporary multiculturalism has rendered old-fashioned Britishness a racist notion while nationalists from England as well as Scotland and Wales have been trumpeting their separateness. To compound the sense of *fin de siècle*, polemics have appeared from right and left with funereal titles like *The Abolition of Britain* and *The Day Britain Died*.[1]

The debate about who we are is alive in our literature, our media and our politics. The confusion was perfectly illustrated during the 1997 election campaign when a series of Conservative party political broadcasts featured an English lion, weeping because it had been tamed by the European Union, while one of Labour's starred a British bulldog, waking after years of slumber.

Less than a decade ago, John Major famously insisted that 'fifty years from now, Britain will still be the country of long shadows on county cricket grounds, warm beer, invincible green suburbs, dog lovers, and – as George Orwell said – old maids bicycling to Holy Communion through the morning mist'.[2] Major's certainty, which was widely mocked at the time, has been challenged head on by his heirs in the Tory Party. Questions of identity dominated the opening skirmishes of the 2001 election campaign after one backbencher alleged that 'our homogenous Anglo-Saxon society has been seriously undermined by the massive immigration, particularly coloured immigration, that has taken place since the war';[3] he went on to complain that this meant the British are becoming 'a mongrel race'.[4] Much of the blame for this row was placed at the door of Major's successor as Conservative leader, William Hague, who was earlier accused of pushing similar buttons by raging against 'bogus asylum seekers' and venturing that Britain is turning into 'a foreign land'.[5]

Against those who want to cling to a traditional definition of Britishness, Major's replacement as prime minister, Tony Blair, has been accused of wanting to set the clock back to year zero; at the very least he has been identified with a number of initiatives to modernise our perception of ourselves. When he was elected party leader he said he aimed to build not just New Labour but also New Britain, and he has subsequently called for the rebirth of a 'young country', been associated with 'Cool Britannia' and established a taskforce to rebrand our national identity.

The only common ground seems to be acknowledgement of the overwhelming evidence that we have lost our shared swagger. There is certainly no agreement on why or what – if anything – should be done about it.

## The end of Britain?

One possible answer to our supposed identity crisis is provided by those who believe that the very concept of a national identity is no longer a useful vehicle for binding our people together. Those who would welcome the end of Britain argue that nations were only ever 'imagined communities', summoned by the 'invention of tradition', without which political leaders could not garner popular acquiescence for their objectives.[6] They suggest that rather than

defending a moribund notion of Britishness, we should
encourage loyalty to either smaller or larger units that can
better serve our needs in the modern world.

The central premise is that the idea of Britain, with its
pretensions to an all-embracing identity, is nothing more
than the eighteenth- and nineteenth-century fabrication of a
dominant English elite that was anxious to suppress Welsh
and Scottish diversity, a construction that is now inevitably
beginning to collapse.

After the Reformation in 1536, Protestantism set the English apart, not just from the Catholic Continental countries
but also from the Nonconformist Welsh and especially the
Catholic Scots. It was to defend the Protestant succession
that Great Britain was suddenly born in the 1707 Act of
Union, which linked England and Wales to Scotland in one
United Kingdom. It was designed by the English to prevent
the Scots from opting for the old Catholicising Stuart
claimants to the united throne rather than accepting a new
Protestant dynasty imported from Hanover, following the
death of childless Queen Anne. Unlike in France or Spain for
example, there was therefore no lengthy process of nation-
building, merely a deliberate attempt to engineer common
loyalties – through symbols like the Union Jack and the
National Anthem – to protect the expansionist ambitions of
the English from what they saw as the rebellious tendencies
of the Scots.

Protestantism subsequently formed an island-wide bond
against the Catholic European powers – notably against
Spain, where the Inquisition persisted throughout the eighteenth century, and against France, which began persecuting
Huguenots after 1688. The rivalry with France was particularly important to the formation of Britishness. The abusive

term 'perfidious Albion' was coined as early as 1652, and from 1689 until 1815 the two countries were almost constantly at war. Mutual suspicion was fed by repeated French support for the Scottish Jacobite challenge on behalf of the exiled Stuarts, and this antagonism was compounded by the French Revolution and ferocious competition for imperial dominance across the globe.

The most comprehensive and influential revisionist history of this process is by Linda Colley in her seminal work *Britons: Forging the Nation, 1707–1837*. She reasons that once France was established as a clear enemy, a 'hostile Other' as she puts it, it was easy for Britons to decide who they were by reference to who they were not. She assumes that 'we can plausibly regard Great Britain as an invented nation superimposed, if only for a while, onto much older alignments and loyalties' such as those to Wales and Scotland.[7] And she reckons that these older loyalties are currently beginning to pull free of the unifying straitjacket because the binds of Britain are weakening. 'The Other in the shape of militant Catholicism, or a hostile Continental European power, or an exotic overseas empire is no longer available to make Britons feel that – by contrast – they have an identity in common,' she concludes.[8]

This is precisely the sentiment that Scottish nationalists have been trying to rouse since the end of the 1970s. Just before the 1979 referendum on home rule, the writer Tom Nairn titled his influential eulogy for Scottish independence *The Break-up of Britain*. Following the 1997 referendum he became sufficiently confident to call his revised assessment *After Britain*.[9]

The belief that Britain may be coming apart has also animated the voices of English nationalism. Conservative leaders have flirted with plans for an English Parliament and the polemical columnist Simon Heffer has gone even further. He advises the English to welcome Scottish devolution as the slip road to the end of the Union and 'the recreation of national identity and the reinvention of England as an independent and proud nation'.[10]

It is true that the identities of the Scots and the Welsh have recently been reinvigorated. This was partly spurred as a reaction against the over-centralisation of Britain and the predominantly English arrogance of British rule, particularly under Margaret Thatcher. It is also the case that signs of Englishness have lately re-emerged: in 1995 the greeting cards company Clinton's began producing tokens to celebrate St George's Day and during the Euro 96 football championships St George's flags suddenly dominated the crowds, normalising the symbol of English nationalism. This in turn was largely a response to Scottish and Welsh claims for recognition. But there is no reason to suppose that a small minority of separatists will persuade the vast majority of Britons that we are stronger apart than together.

Liberating these expressions of allegiance was the very point of devolution, without which pent-up anger at their suffocation would have increased hostility to Britain. The Conservative and Unionist Party, in evincing a lack of respect for Scottish and Welsh sensibilities, came to stand for England first and the Union second; their intransigence fomented resentment – symbolised by the struggle over the poll tax – which helps to explain why they did not win a single Scottish or Welsh constituency in 1997 and why they clawed back just one Scottish seat in 2001.

There is a legitimate English question – where does England fit into the reconfiguration of Britain? – but it is an issue for debate not a reason to break up the Union. While there are nationalists and populists who seek to prey on hopes or fears that devolution is the glide path to independence, support for separatism has actually abated since the introduction of the Welsh Assembly and the Scottish Parliament. In the 2001 election Plaid Cymru made no net gains while the Scottish National Party suffered a collapse of its vote. The fact is that British ties have been loosened not severed and in the process they have been fortified.

Those who believe that Britishness can no longer envelop such diversity are not the only ones to argue that the current debate about who we are will lead to the end of Britain. There is also a small band of European centralists who argue that we should seek rejuvenation by willingly subsuming ourselves in a wider European 'superstate', which is what they hope the European Union will become.

One of the most articulate agitators for Britain to be taken over by Europe is the academic and political activist Stephen Haseler, who supposes that 'the state, and even the nation, have not for some time been adequate, or desirable, objects of loyalty and affection'.[11] Hence, he predicts, 'we are now coming to the end of the British story'.[12] He argues that government in a place the size of Britain is ineffective because it is both too large to permit a genuine spirit of community and too small to protect people from the forces of globalisation. He therefore proselytises for the abolition of Britain and 'the absorption of the UK state into the European Union'.[13]

These European centralists, though tiny in number and with almost no purchase on public opinion, have caused a huge stir in the debate about Britishness. They appear even more threatening than the separatists because they suppose that not only have Britons lost affection for the nation but also that there is an external agency willing and able to take us over. But they are wrong on both counts. As we shall see later, the European Union is not, and will not become, the 'superstate' they desire. And in any case there is plenty of proof that the nation still inspires widespread loyalty and affection; in this respect it is intriguing that Scottish nationalists tend to be keen on European integration in the certainty that it would not suffocate their national identity in the way they believe that Britain does.

Even if the concept of Britishness was originally foisted on the Welsh and the Scots by an English core soon after 1707, the seeds have long since taken root. It is fallacious to deduce that the recent absence of a 'hostile Other' has wiped out the past three centuries of nation-building. There now certainly is such a thing as Britain that stands proudly and distinctly from other European countries.

A recent *Social Attitudes Survey* revealed that the vast majority of Britons feel more closely attached to Britain than to any of its component nations, or to their county, town or neighbourhood, or to Europe. This affinity is not uncritical but it clearly runs deep: while three-quarters agreed that 'there are some things about Britain today that make me ashamed', an even larger proportion expressed pride in Britain. This strength of feeling was far greater than in any of the other Western European countries studied.[14]

There has even been a resurgence in many of the symbols of Britishness.[15] Most notably the Union Jack, no more the preserve of racist groups and football hooligans, has been reclaimed and reborn as a proud icon. It was worn on Ginger Spice's micro-dress at the Brit Awards, on Liam Gallagher's bed-sheets for the cover of *Vanity Fair*, and on Prince

William's waistcoat in the official photographs released by Buckingham Palace to mark his eighteenth birthday. Furthermore, the 'British' prefix increasingly adds international value to our products. That is true of Brit Art, Britpop, British literature, British film, British advertising, British design, British fashion and British architecture. Britain leads the world in creative industries, the cultural motors that help to define our national identity at home and abroad.

Britain is secure. But Britishness is evolving into something less defensive and more pluralist. There is no longer a 'hostile Other' – despite attempts to recreate one in the shape of the European Union – forcing us together as if we were clinging to a liferaft. There is no longer an English elite suppressing Welsh and Scottish characteristics. Instead, for most people there is an exciting recognition that after three hundred years and more of shared experiences we are united enough to appreciate that Britons are not uniformly the same.

Most of us are learning that identities are not like hats which can be worn only one at a time; they are like badges that can be displayed in any combination. The majority of Britons are increasingly acknowledging the possibility, even the desirability, of multiple identities, and this is forging a unique series of concentric circles of loyalty. For example, those football fans who cheer Celtic over Rangers no doubt share a Glaswegian rivalry against Edinburgh; at the same time both cities come together in support of Scotland's rugby team against England's; simultaneously the Scots, English and Welsh are joined in wanting British athletes to win gold medals at the Olympics; and with the French and Germans we all back the Europeans against the Americans in golf's Ryder Cup.

Britishness is becoming more diverse and more inclusive, accommodating not just Welsh, Scottish and Irish ties, but those of other groups too. Race riots in Burnley, Oldham and other cities in 2001 – often accompanied by high votes for the British National Party in those places – were the extreme reaction of an intolerant minority to our emerging multiethnic and multicultural country. But the almost universal outrage at the murder of Stephen Lawrence, and the burgeoning of the Notting Hill Carnival into an event enjoyed by many from outside the Afro-Caribbean community, show that while there are still pockets of terrible prejudice ethnic minorities are becoming integral to the national culture. Black-Britons have emerged as role models in the media, politics and sport, and British-Asians are finally breaking out of curry house and corner shop stereotypes with the success of the Asian Dub Foundation pop band, the *Goodness Gracious Me* television comedy and the *East Is East* hit film.

This does not mean that Britain is segregating into numerous minority communities either. Far from it, they are integrating into the whole. Black-Britons and British-Asians tend not to identify with particular parts of Britain, which they often see as too ethnically exclusive, but want to belong to Britain itself. The commentator Yasmin Alibhai-Brown, in her book *Who Do We Think We Are?*, explains that she does not feel herself to be English but British. She is hostile to the break-up of Britain because it would leave her without a home, hypothetically asking 'when Scotland has got kilted up and the English have established their homelands far from the Welsh and Irish, where do we, the black Britons, go?'[16]

The vast bulk of Britain is becoming knowingly heterogeneous, a compound of people who can each cherish distinct identities. This makes the whole greater than the sum of its parts. We are all minorities now, except as Britons. This profound realisation partly explains why it is so hard to define what it means to be British. The current crisis is not of British national identity but of those who refuse to see the strength in our diversity: those European centralists who would have Britain swallowed by a fictitious 'superstate', those Scottish and Welsh separatists who have failed to win support for a break-away, and more especially those Little Englanders who are losing their stultifying supremacy.

## Anti-Europeans

While the views of European centralists are given much greater prominence than their small numbers warrant, the debate about Britishness has become dominated by what appears to be their polar opposite: those who are convinced that the European Union is the modern incarnation of a 'hostile Other', the leading aggressor that threatens to destroy an idea of Britain to which they are strongly attached.

Stripped of grace words, their argument runs something like this: that fourteen other countries have ganged together, largely under Franco-German leadership, to forge a European 'superstate', of which a single currency is the final piece in the jigsaw, that is more or less dedicated to destroying the traditional British way of life. Almost their sole solution to our supposed identity crisis is therefore to beat back encroachment by 'Brussels'.

There are subtle differences between these anti-Europeans, however, because they are not all trying to defend the same idea of Britain. For convenience, they can be divided into four general categories.

### Old-fashioned socialists

The origins of contemporary anti-European socialism can be dated precisely to 3 October 1962, when Hugh Gaitskell, the Labour leader, famously denounced Harold Macmillan, the Conservative Prime Minister, for his application for Britain to join the Common Market. Many Labour figures since the Second World War had been hostile to British involvement in Europe, but none found such uncompromising demagoguery as Gaitskell, who lectured the party conference that membership would mean 'the end of Britain as an independent European state' and 'the end of a thousand years of history'.

It was a turning point for Labour. Gaitskell dismayed and weakened his natural reformist supporters, who were led by Roy Jenkins. Jenkins's chief rivals inevitably used the speech to slip into arguing that Europe was at best unimportant and at worst dangerous. By splintering the moderates, and by providing a populist anti-European rallying cry, Gaitskell unleashed the disparate forces of Euro-scepticism that dogged the party for a quarter of a century.

Gaitskell himself was primarily concerned that joining the European Economic Community might impair the Commonwealth. This was a major worry throughout the 1960s and 1970s not just for Conservatives but for many in the Labour Party too, including Harold Wilson, Gaitskell's successor, who initially resisted the turn to Europe with another philippic. 'We are not entitled to sell our friends and kinsmen down the river for a problematical and marginal advantage in selling washing machines in Düsseldorf,' he said in 1961.

Others had different phobias. Denis Healey had long thought that Continental Catholicism had stripped Social Democrat parties of their socialist ideology, rendering them

ineffective allies. Barbara Castle championed the idea that the
EEC was a capitalist cartel, opposed to state intervention and
dominated by Christian Democrat governments. And more
bluntly Richard Crossman recorded in his diary that 'I regard
Little England as the pre-condition for any successful socialist planning'.[17]

This struggle for socialism in one country became the
dominant theme of Labour anti-Marketeers during the
1970s and 1980s. After Britain finally entered the Community in 1973, Michael Foot told the party conference that
their election manifesto could not promise to 'carry out a full
socialist policy unless there is provision also for the Treaty of
Accession to be torn up'.[18] Peter Shore reiterated the point.
'If we are not prepared to renegotiate, if we are not prepared
to break and to withdraw,' he said, 'then you can roll up the
map of democratic socialism not for these ten years but for
the whole future as far ahead as we can see; because we shall
be entering an organisation where frankly our cause is heavily outnumbered'.[19]

In the run-up to the referendum in 1975, Tony Benn took
the argument back to where Gaitskell had begun and made
the issue one of constitutional principle. He claimed that
continued membership threatened the 1688 constitutional
settlement and would 'mean the end of Britain as a completely self-governing nation and of our democratically
elected Parliament as the supreme law-making body of the
United Kingdom'.[20]

What united these views was the fear that cooperation in
a 'bosses's Europe' would inhibit Labour and the trade unions
from creating the kind of Britain they wanted. Although
these socialist anti-Marketeers were never strong enough to
disrupt Britain's place in Europe, they did succeed in first

splitting then controlling the Labour Party. Wilson was unable to prevent half a dozen Cabinet ministers from campaigning in the 1975 referendum for a No vote, contrary to the recommendation of the Government. The party conference voted in 1980 for a policy of withdrawal, a decision cited by Jenkins and the Gang of Four as a major reason for their defection to establish the SDP. And by 1983 Labour's manifesto-cum-suicide note declared that 'withdrawal from the Community is the right policy for Britain – to be completed well within the lifetime of the next Parliament'.

After years of rising Euro-phobia – and, incidentally, years in the wilderness of opposition – Neil Kinnock finally began to force the party to recognise reality. He, then John Smith and Tony Blair, embarked on a programme of modernisation that included the embrace of pro-European policies. Although a handful of the old guard still keeps the flag flying, with the support of the *Morning Star* and the Socialist Workers' Party, old-fashioned socialist anti-Europeans are now very few and far between. Their voices are barely heard these days, drowned out by the din made by those in the conservative establishment.

### Fogeys

There is a strong strand of nostalgia in the politics of contemporary High Tories that traces its lineage through John Major's remarks about 'warm beer' back to Stanley Baldwin's famous address, 'On England', in 1924. 'The sounds of England, the tinkle of the hammer on the anvil in the country smithy, the corncrake on a dewy morning, the sound of the scythe against the whetstone, and the sight of a plough team coming over the brow of a hill, the sight that has been seen in England since England was a land, and may be seen in

England long after the Empire has perished and every works in England has ceased to function, for centuries the one eternal sight of England,' predicted the Conservative Prime Minister.[21] Yet this romantic picture obviously does not describe modern Britain; in fact it was obsolete even before it was drawn, since by the 1920s England had already been predominantly urban for seventy years.

It is important that much of this sentimental attachment is not really to Britain at all, but to England. And certainly not to England as it is, but to a place they believe there was, and even that was enjoyed only by a tiny elite. The *Peter Simple* column in *The Daily Telegraph* has been grieving for this lost world since it originally appeared in 1955. A good example was published soon after the 1997 election. 'In the past 50 years they [the English] have seen everything that is distinctively English suppressed and derided. They have seen all the evils that flow from the gutters of America – vile entertainment, degenerate pop music, feminism, "political correctness" – infect their country. They have seen their decent manners and customs corrupted. They have seen sexual deviance elevated in official esteem and even officially commended. They have seen parts of their country colonised by immigrants and been forbidden by law to speak freely of the consequences.'[22]

Rolling back the years has been the aim of *This England* magazine since it was launched in 1968 under the slogan 'as refreshing as a cup of tea!' with the promise to 'capture the true spirit of England in every edition'. An editorial in the summer of 1997 made clear where it believes the threat to this true spirit comes from. 'We are in the middle of a carefully crafted plot going back many years which is designed to create an easily manageable, European superstate to be run like a socialist republic,' it warned. 'Our precious Monarchy will be replaced by a President on the Continent, the Union Jack will be banned in favour of that horrid blue rag with those 12 nasty yellow stars and we shall all have to sing the new Euro anthem to the tune of Beethoven's Ode to Joy,' it added, 'except that the title will really mean "Goodbye Britain".'[23]

This valediction has echoed through a mountain of recent books. Linda Proud and Valerie Petts (*Consider England*), Peter Vansittart (*In Memory of England*), Roger Scruton (*England: An Elegy*) and Richard Body (*England for the English*) tell their tales in their titles.[24] Clive Aslet, the editor of *Country Life*, reported in his confused panegyric to the past, *Anyone for England? A Search for British Identity*, that 'day and night the ogres of Brussels can be heard stamping about the corridors of the European Union, as their cry of "Fee, fie, fo, fum, I smell the traditional habits, tastes and foodstuffs of an Englishman" reverberates across the Channel'.[25]

The ultimate fortress of this exclusive nostalgia against Europe and the modern world is *The Spectator*. Ian Buruma, a staff correspondent throughout the 1990s, has written a wonderful vignette of the magazine's theatrical camp.[26] He says its office, a fine Georgian house in Bloomsbury, is like a stage decorated by receptionists with cut-glass accents and old or at least long family names, and its principal journalists are 'a bit like characters in an old play which has gone through too many revivals'. And his portrait of the then editor Charles Moore, 'he looked and spoke like a man from an almost vanished world,' could equally apply to his successors. Their fogeyish life of quixotic illusions and eccentric affectations is, he writes, all about 'old money, old schools, old families, old silver and old gentlemanly wit'. But old now seems old-fashioned and out of place in a meritocracy.

The England they love, the *ancien régime*, is fading away. So it is no wonder they feel like 'strangers in our own land', as the Conservative intellectual David Willets put it.[27] The Earl of Burford illustrates their problem. Waiting to inherit a more noble title, it must have been very hard for him – Charles Francis Topham de Vere Beauclerk, a descendent of Charles II and his mistress Nell Gwyn – to accept that most hereditary peers were finally to be expelled from the House of Lords in 1999; which is presumably why during the vote he broke into the Chamber, leapt onto the Woolsack and shouted 'this Bill, drafted in Brussels, is Treason; what we are witnessing is the abolition of Britain'.

As Britain evolves, militant fogeys like the Earl of Burford – who has since joined the tiny Democratic Party to campaign against 'Brussels' – are bitterly trying to consecrate a country that bares scant resemblance to that inhabited by most people. Their England is based on birth and privilege not effort and merit. Their England is idyllically rural not messily urban: although they may own town houses in leafy London, they imagine the pastures of Kent to be their front lawn while their back garden stretches little further than what is quaintly called the Home Counties.

Through this distorted perspective they would turn aspects of our popular identity into the kind of tourist theme park that was recently parodied by Julian Barnes in his novel *England, England*.[28] This is the place where Beefeaters, Big Ben and Buckingham Palace are marketed for common consumption on biscuit tin lids. If they had their way, our country would be left like a crumbling stately home, a museum of Ye Olde England, open to visitors who admire nothing so much as its age and its coat of arms.

As Britain diversifies, as economic and political progress

challenges the old vested interests, those who fear they are
losing control inevitably lash out to try to protect their position. They are determined to preserve the past. And they are
desperate for someone to blame for the march of time. For
them, the foremost scapegoat has become the European
Union.

### Thatcherites

It is ironic that few have done as much to tear down the
*ancien régime* as the heroine of modern Conservatism,
Margaret Thatcher. In liberating middle-class aspirations,
teaching that profit not privilege most deserves respect, she
ripped apart many of the institutions and much of the culture that had sustained the old order. Yet those still stuck to
Thatcherism also fear that their country – the place they created in their own image during the 1980s – is under assault
too. They had no qualms about European integration, despite
the implications for national sovereignty it entailed, when
they believed it was an ally in their project. Almost all the
current Conservative anti-Europeans supported entry into
the Community in 1973, when the principle of pooled sovereignty was established, and virtually none was against the
Single European Act in 1986, the single greatest act of integration, because they thought Europe would bolster the
free-market revolution.

Since the late 1980s, however, Jacques Delors, the Social
Chapter and the single currency have convinced them that
Europe has become an aggressive adversary of Thatcherism.
After all, they point out, there are no leading Conservatives
in Europe, just Christian Democrats. Mirroring the views
of the socialist anti-Marketeers of the 1960s and 1970s,
Thatcherites now want to pull down the shutters against

Europe as they fear it will somehow prevent them from nursing the kind of Britain they started to build in the 1980s. Hence, they now claim to be trapped in an emerging 'superstate' that is committed to overthrowing their revolution.

Befitting a grocer's daughter who led a nation of shopkeepers, an emblem of identity for Thatcherites might be John Bull. The pugnacious cartoon tradesman was invented in 1712, just after the birth of Britain, and survived as a national symbol until our finest hour, the Second World War. According to his creator, the beer-swilling, beef-eating John Bull was 'an honest, plain dealing fellow, choleric, bold and of a very unconstant temper' who fiercely defended his freedom from the Continentals, notably Nicholas Frog, 'especially if they pretended to govern him'.[29] It is this invincible attitude that Thatcherites summon in their crusade to stop 'Brussels' from crushing our individualism, entrepreneurial economics and liberal democracy.

It is evident in the Dunkirk spirit and Battle of Britain metaphors they constantly deploy. It lay behind Michael Portillo's outburst at a Conservative Party conference, when the then Defence Secretary swore 'around the world three letters send a chill down the spine of the enemy: SAS. And those letters spell out one clear message: "don't mess with Britain".'[30] This sentiment bleeds into offensive accusations that modern German democratic politicians are using the European Union as a vehicle to fulfil Hitler's expansionist ambition of taking over Europe and Britain. One of the most recent examples occurred at the beginning of the 2001 election campaign when Conservative backbencher Peter Tapsell alleged that a European single currency was a Nazi idea and that proposals for EU reform outlined by Gerhard Schröder, the German Chancellor, were part of a 'Germanic master plan', adding 'we may not have studied Hitler's *Mein Kampf* in time but, by heaven, there is no excuse for us not studying the Schröder plan now'.[31] This odious thought drips from every page of Andrew Roberts's futuristic novel *The Aachen Memorandum*, in which the right-wing historian depicts the European Union as a Nazi Reich where German functionaries assassinate Margaret Thatcher, rename Waterloo station after Maastricht and punish women who shave their armpits, until they are finally beaten back by the English Resistance Movement.[32]

In real life, some think it may already be too late to save us from 'Brussels'. In his tirade against European integration for inducing *The Death of Britain*, the former Tory Cabinet Minister John Redwood manages to blame Europe for devolution, reforms to the honours system, the lack of respect shown to hereditary peers and the decommissioning of the royal yacht *Britannia*. 'As the United Kingdom will have to adopt more continental ways, there could come a point where people are no longer prepared to obey the Brussels law or might take to the streets to protest when it doesn't suit,' he writes, because 'there is nostalgia and fear in the air as there was on the eve of the First World War'.[33]

For Thatcherites the danger to English exceptionalism from Hitler has been replaced by 'Brussels law', apparently enacted by 'Brussels bureaucrats'. The particular exceptionalism they defend is peculiarly English, however, not British. Its ancestry was controversially traced by Alan Macfarlane in his innovative history *The Origins of English Individualism*, published the year before Thatcher came to power. He argues that a singular respect for personal liberty was deeply embedded in England long before a taste for freedom was acquired on the Continent, because even before the Black Death in

1350 property rights were enshrined in law. He concludes that 'the majority of ordinary people in England from at least the thirteenth century were rampant individualists, highly mobile both geographically and socially, economically "rational", market-oriented and acquisitive, ego-centred in kinship and social life' and 'not based on either "Community" or "communities"'.[34] He adds that this consciousness has been uniquely exalted in our national identity ever since, putting us at odds with the socialistic Europeans.

This theory, regardless of its historical inaccuracies, has become the intellectual justification for the belated Thatcherite frenzy against Europe. William Hague carried the baton with gusto. The Britishness he defined was conveniently compatible with the values he hoped to resonate from the Conservative Party, going so far as to praise Macfarlane and claim that 'Thatcherism pre-dated Margaret Thatcher by eight hundred years'.[35] It was also diametrically opposed to the principles he allotted to the European Union, which was portrayed as the back door to socialism. Ergo the one must be defended from the other. 'If you believe in an independent Britain,' he declaimed, in an echo of Hugh Gaitskell and Tony Benn, 'then come with me, and I will give you back your country.'[36]

It is this spirit that has led the Tory Party into more and more extreme postures and further from the realities of dealing with Europe, a position from which they show no sign of retreating. This is in stark contrast to the attitude of Conservatives in government, from Harold Macmillan through to and including Margaret Thatcher, who understood the need to work with our European partners not shout at them from afar.

*Chauvinists*

Patriots, as Samuel Johnson noted, are simply people who love their country. And British patriotism, which rightly runs deep, expresses itself in many ways. Harold Wilson famously benefited from the euphoria that followed England's World Cup win in 1966, and his surprise defeat in the 1970 election is often attributed to the fact that England were knocked out of the World Cup four days earlier. More importantly, when Britain endured a rain of bombs at the height of the Blitz in 1940, standing alone after the fall of France and before the Nazi invasion of Russia, patriotic fervour helped pull our country through its darkest hour.

During the Second World War Winston Churchill's speeches and Vera Lynn's songs helped to crystallise the solidarity of the British people in the fight against an evil enemy. So did George Orwell's *The Lion and the Unicorn*, which has since often been cited as the set-text for patriots. On its opening page, Orwell lauded our 'overwhelming strength of patriotism', noting that 'as a *positive* force there is nothing to set beside it'.[37] He was right, and this strength has repeatedly helped our country survive in times of crisis. Our patriotism is no less important when there is no Battle of Britain, no 'hostile Other', because we still need a mutual understanding of the challenges we face and a combined effort to take the country forward to shared aims.

However, some people conflate patriotism with irrational nationalism, which can spill over into bellicose jingoism or outright racism. Both patriotism and nationalism rest on the recognition of difference, on the distinction between what is British and what is not; but one is positive, the other destructive. By Charles de Gaulle's definition, 'patriotism is when love of your own people comes first; nationalism is when hate for people other than your own comes first'.[38] Such chauvinism is not drawn from Orwell but from visceral prejudice, where pride turns to conceit, where our history is wielded as an excuse to bash the French and the Dunkirk spirit degenerates into anti-German hysteria.

Behind this bogus patriotism lurks xenophobic bigotry. It is the last refuge of politicians who set support of the English cricket team as a test of national fidelity and of journalists who indiscriminately scatter offence towards the French and the Germans for a cheap headline. And it is the driving force behind football hooligans who cloak their violence in the Flag of St George, almost certainly unaware that George never once set foot in England or that he is also the patron saint of Aragon and Portugal as well as the protector of Genoa and Venice.

This arrogant ignorance is informed by the romantic history of the 'Island Story', legends of heroism perpetuated in popular culture by the likes of Arthur Bryant and *Dad's Army*. Such insularity is wonderfully ridiculed by the American Anglophile Bill Bryson in his best-selling satire *Notes From A Small Island*. He derides the 'shared pretence that Britain is a lonely island in the middle of an empty green sea,' suggesting that 'if your concept of world geography was shaped entirely by what you read in the papers and saw on television, you would have no choice but to conclude that America must be about where Ireland is, that France and Germany lie roughly alongside the Azores' and that 'pretty much all the other sovereign states are either mythical' or 'can only be reached by spaceship'.[39] It is this sense of perspective that leads some to stick their heads in the sand and simply blame 'foreigners' for all their troubles.

The true set-text for chauvinists is not Orwell, but

W. C. Sellar and R. J. Yeatman. Their famous parody, *1066 And All That*, opens by arguing 'the Norman Conquest was a Good Thing, as from this time onwards England stopped being conquered and thus was able to become top nation'.[40] Its final verdict is that the First World War was a Bad Thing because 'America was thus clearly top nation and History came to a .'[41] Insecure chauvinists have struggled to come to terms with that full stop ever since.

All these groups are clearly worried that their version of Britishness is slipping away. Contrary to their avowed inter-nationalism, old-fashioned socialists are cowed that they cannot construct their vision of society without the protec-tion of the moat that defends them from the rest of the world; fogeys despair at the overthrow of their *ancien régime*; Thatcherites fear for their 1980s legacy; and chauvinists are simply rancorous to foreigners. And all have rediscovered a 'hostile Other' in the shape of the European Union, which they imagine to be a 'superstate' waiting to plunder their par-tisan version of our thousand years of history. Their fight to entrench these sectional definitions of national identity, and their battle to protect them from this invented enemy, is another part of the reason for the current confusion over what it means to be British.

Although they hate to admit it, these groups have much in common with each other because they are all resistant to changes that might diminish their power and influence. They have much in common with European centralists as well because they too cannot foresee a diverse and inclusive Britishness emerging that is stronger than the one they know. A supposed 'superstate' is for one side the problem and for the other the solution. But this has left the argument about Britain's relations with Europe hideously polarised, with the mainstream common-sense majority left understandably confused and alarmed.

## Britishness

Britain's national identity is neither fake – it no more exists solely in contrast to a 'hostile Other' than do the images conjured by those patriots who revere 'the American dream' or '*La France*' – nor fossilised – it has never been set in stone but has constantly evolved as it passes down the generations. While England has been dominant in Britain – today 85 per cent of Britons are English – our bond is obviously informed by a cross-fertilisation of Welsh and Scottish experiences too. These days 20 per cent of people living in Wales were born in England and 15 per cent of people born in Scotland now live in England. This fuzzy rapport – further blurred by incorporating immigrant Irish and Commonwealth influences – has allowed our separate loyalties to flourish while still differentiating us all from other European countries, just as they differ from each other.

Britishness has been shaped by a common consciousness beyond that of its component groups. The seeds may have been sown by the English ruling classes in the middle of the eighteenth century, when institutions like the British Museum and the *Encyclopaedia Britannica* were founded. But it took on a life of its own as all the people of the island, regardless of their class and other differences, built the nation together. The seminal moments in this process were the forging of the Industrial Revolution, the establishing and ruling of the Empire, and most especially the victories over aggressors from Europe in two World Wars. All these were undoubtedly British not English endeavours.

The advent of Britain liberated economic activity because the Act of Union abolished domestic trade barriers and encouraged transport and communication networks to reach into all parts of the country, opening markets, stimulating internal migration and bringing the regions closer together. Coal mining, steelworking and shipbuilding flourished in South Wales and the central belt of Scotland, as Britain not England became the workshop of the world. And after the loss of the American colonies in 1783, Britons pulled together to expand the Empire. Explorers, sailors and soldiers, manufacturers and traders, engineers and governor generals were Welsh and Scottish as well as English, and Glasgow rightly claimed to be the second city of an Empire that covered more than a quarter of the world.

On the one hand, this ascendancy fostered a liberal Britishness. The Battle of Waterloo was certainly not won only on the playing fields of Eton, and military successes led to reforms that spread the spoils beyond the upper classes. The embrace of national identity was broadened as Britain emancipated Catholics and extended the franchise to include the middle and working classes and eventually women too. On the other hand, as Britannia ruled the waves during the Victorian period, Britishness was also imbued with an air of elitism. Public schools, recast on Thomas Arnold's brutal model at Rugby, invented games and created gentlemen but also instilled deference and repression; the honours system was expanded, enlarging the aristocracy; and the monarchy adopted extravagant ceremonials. Meanwhile a current of racial supremacy emerged: Rudyard Kipling was not alone in calling on the 'half devil and half child' in the colonies to 'take up the White Man's burden' and 'serve your captive's need'.

This British feeling of superiority appeared to be confirmed by victory in the Great War. It was then challenged and utterly vindicated by the Second World War. United, but almost alone in Europe, Britain defended everything it had come to stand for in a fight for survival against the evils of Nazism. That concept of Britishness was seared into our collective psyche by the flames of conflict, as Britons understood more clearly than ever what it meant to be British.

This defining picture of Britishness has cast a long and dark shadow over the debate about who we are today. This ideal, of a country winning through against all the odds to beat back a terrible threat from the Continent to our liberty and even our existence, has restricted our ability to change with the times. Instead of continuing to develop as it had done in the past, our perception of ourselves appears to have been pickled in that glorious moment. In consequence, we have often made the wrong choices for our country, failing to properly advance our national interests in the changed context of the modern world; we have failed to heed Winston Churchill's famous warning that those who build the present only in the image of the past will miss out altogether on the challenges of the future. By pretending that we can still go it alone, or rely solely on the United States, standing in isolation from our nearest neighbours and biggest trading partners, we have too often cut ourselves off from developments in Europe that directly impact upon us.

It is not 1945. The world is different now. Globalisation is bringing us all closer together. Nuclear weapons, criminals and terrorists do not respect national borders. International finance regularly disrupts national economies. Multinational corporations, often with budgets larger than those of countries, frequently circumvent national governments. Worldwide 24-hour mass communications are homogenising cultures. And cuts in the Amazon rainforest drill holes in the ozone layer that pollute the environment across the planet.

Britain does not have the same role in the world either. The end of Empire, the rise of the US, relative economic decline and the resurgence of occupied or defeated European countries have all pulled us down the league of nations.

In fact, in the past fifty years Britain itself has been transformed. This is reflected in our changing attitudes to institutions like Parliament, the monarchy and the church, as well as by the confusion in our culture. Five decades after 492 Jamaican immigrants stepped off the *Empire Windrush* at Tilbury, Britain is multiethnic and multicultural: Black-Britons, British-Asians, Jews, Irish and others with recent roots outside the island now compose just under 10 per cent of the population and up to 30 per cent in some inner-city areas. Rock 'n' roll liberated the teenager in the 1950s and 1960s, promoting a powerful youth culture that is today epitomised by the ubiquity of dance music. Demands for equality by women from the 1970s and homosexuals from the 1980s have significantly impacted on domestic and working life, and the explosion of education, technology and income levels is breaking down class barriers.

Radical changes to Britain, to Britain's role in the world, and to the world itself, are profound challenges to our Second World War identity. Our sense of superiority has finally been damaged by the unpalatable realities we see all around us. Yet Britishness was so sharply defined and so deeply embedded in 1945 that we have not fully come to terms with all these confusing realities, and we often seem to be stuck in a finest hour that is more than half a century out of date. We frequently have the attitudes, but rarely the authority, of the Great Power we once were. This mismatch underpins all the uncertainty about what it means to be British these days.

Confidence will return only once we agree how to deal with these changes in Britain's condition. Neither European centralists – because they eschew patriotism – nor anti-Europeans – because they are longing for a lost past that merely served their sectional interests – can offer a lead. Running away from Britain or stoking traditional fears of Europe is no way to advance our national interests in the turbulent twenty-first century. The effect of their wishful thinking or scaremongering has simply been to make it fashionable to blame the European Union for the fact that Britain looks different today than in 1945. They are both letting Britain down by spreading false fears about the future.

The European Union cannot damage our national identity. If Britishness were so fragile it would hardly be worth defending. This argument raged during the 1975 referendum campaign on Britain's membership of the EEC, when the best point was put most forcefully by none other than *The Sun*. 'Are the French a soupçon less French? Are the Germans a sauerkraut less German? Are the Italians a pizza less Italian? Of course they are not! And neither would Britain be any less British,' it correctly asserted in a thumping leader.[42]

Britain's national identity is not under threat from Europe. Our confidence has been impaired because our own awareness of ourselves has failed to keep pace with the times. Modern Britain is breaking through in our culture and struggling for representation in our institutions against those who are determined to turn back the clock. Our national identity must evolve as it has throughout history or it will ossify and atrophy. If Britons do not feel that they have a stake in our future then we will not pull together, we will drift apart, because there will be no agreement on the way ahead. And if our national ambitions are unrealistic, they will run into the sand. We will take decisions based on a fantasy that actually do us damage in the real world.

Britons do face a choice, but it is not between defending ourselves from Europe and swapping our country for a 'superstate'. Either we can become prisoners of our past, shrinking into an insular nationalism, frightened of foreigners and the future. Or we can accept that we have changed since 1945 and need to find modern models, perhaps less palatable to many of us than in the past, for advancing our national interests in the age of globalisation.

# The Fear of Europe

## Britain and Europe, 1945–73

Long after the Second World War British leaders continued
to believe that our unique role as a Great Power came at the
intersection of three circles of influence: the Commonwealth, the United States and Europe. Maintaining Imperial
links and searching for a 'special relationship' with the US,
important though they were, became such dominant priorities that the prevailing consensus was blinkered to the
emerging centrality of Europe. Meanwhile, stuttering economic performance led Britain to slip behind first West
Germany, then France and later Italy in the European peck-
ing order.

The Empire took more than two centuries to build and
less than two decades to dismantle. The sun began to set on
British territory in 1947 but politicians as diverse as Anthony
Eden and Hugh Gaitskell clung to the hope after 1949 that
the Commonwealth would sustain our global reach. So their

overriding objectives were protecting colonial trade and pre-
serving the sterling area. Yet the truth was captured by Dean
Acheson, the US Secretary of State, who coined the famous
aphorism that 'Great Britain has lost an empire and has not
yet found a role.'[1]

The role that many sought was at the side of the United
States. Even after the humiliation of Suez in 1956, which dis-
turbed Britain's assumptions about both the Commonwealth
and the US, developments in Europe were still ignored.
The Americans themselves were perplexed. Acheson voiced
Washington orthodoxy by observing that 'the attempt to play
a separate power role, that is, a role apart from Europe, a role
based primarily on a "special relationship" with the United
States, a role based on being head of the Commonwealth, is
about played out'.[2]

The attempt to play a role apart from Europe was bolstered by another blind spot, the delusion of economic
might. The costs of war were huge – a quarter of the national
wealth was lost, proportionately more than any other com-
batant – and Britain was left with a weakened industrial base,
a colossal trade gap and severely depleted gold and dollar
reserves. It is true that Britain was still stronger than the
defeated and ravaged Continental powers, but this advantage
was soon lost. Between 1947 and 1951 industrial production
in Britain rose by 30 per cent, but by 50 per cent in France
and Italy and 300 per cent in West Germany. At the very
moment when Harold Macmillan told Britons we had never
had it so good, Britain started falling behind. The relative
decline was rapid. In 1914 Britain's national income was just
below that of Germany and almost double that of France; by
the 1980s it was about half that of the FRG, just two-thirds
that of France and less than that of Italy.

Successive governments simply refused to face facts. Henry Tizard, Chief Scientific Adviser at the Ministry of Defence, was almost alone in his assessment of the post-war position. 'We persist in regarding ourselves as a Great Power,' he wrote in 1949, 'capable of everything and only temporarily handicapped by economic difficulties. We are not a Great Power and never will be again. We are a great nation, but if we continue to behave like a Great Power we shall soon cease to be a great nation.'[3]

Acheson, Tizard and others were ignored partly because of the long record of distrust of those across the Channel. The belief that Britain is under threat from Continental tyranny goes back centuries, probably to Julius Caesar's invasion in 55 BC and certainly to the Norman Conquest in 1066. Almost uniquely in Europe, we have suffered no foreign occupation, serious military defeat, civil war or revolutionary upheaval for 250 years, and for lengthy periods ours has been the only major European country with a free press and a freely elected government. By contrast, France has been through one monarchy, two empires and five republics in the past two centuries, while in half that time Germany has swapped from a monarchy to a republic to a Reich, then to partition between capitalism and communism and back to a reunified republic. In the past fifty years, most other people in Western and Eastern Europe have either suffered totalitarian regimes or been invaded and impoverished.

To check the danger, Britain had traditionally tried to maintain the balance of power in Europe while avoiding permanent engagement on the mainland. As Lord Palmerston put it, we had eternal interests – to prevent the Continent uniting against us – but no eternal allies. After the war, however, the balance of power shifted from Britain to

Europe. Lacking faith in the abilities of nation-states, countries ashamed of their recent past were willing to start peacefully uniting their interests. Britain was not, and the condition we had feared for so long was finally brought about: we were left isolated.[4]

This was not the result of aggression by foreign powers, but our own diplomatic and political incompetence. It did not, however, kill off the illusion that Britain could simultaneously lead and remain aloof, so our reaction to continuing European developments repeated a tedious pattern. The immediate response was to dismiss any initiative as virtually meaningless and bound to fail. The next move was to avoid getting sucked into negotiations for fear of being tied to unpalatable outcomes, while agitating for a looser model to rival the original. Then finally we have been compelled to apply for belated membership of clubs where the rules have already been set without taking account of our interests. By letting our fear of Europe hold sway over an objective assessment of our national interests, we have had little or no control over events that have affected us deeply. Unable to find a practicable alternative, we have been reluctant Europeans, forced against our wishes to accept that our future is inexorably linked to an integrating Continent over which we had lost influence.

### The Schuman Plan

On 9 May 1950 Robert Schuman, the French Foreign Minister, unveiled a plan to bring the management of Europe's coal and steel industries, the backbone of manufacturing and military strength, under the control of a supranational High Authority. This audacious initiative was conceived by Jean Monnet, head of the French Economic Planning Commission, who hoped that pooling these resources would become 'the germ of European unity'.[5]

The Schuman Plan was adopted by France as a way of controlling its neighbour's expansion and it was embraced by West Germany as a path back to respectable recovery. Britain's initial attitude was contained in a pair of legendary remarks. Ernest Bevin, the Foreign Secretary, referred to the prospect of Franco-German collaboration by warning 'if you open that Pandora's Box, you never know what Trojan horses will jump out'. And Herbert Morrison, the Deputy Prime Minister, concerned that a cartel of private companies might compromise Britain's newly nationalised coal and steel industries, concluded 'the Durham miners will never wear it'.

Monnet made his view of British participation crystal clear. 'I hope with all my heart that you will join in this from the start,' he said, 'but if you don't, we shall go ahead without you.'[6] This opened a recurring dilemma for Britain. Joining would entail the pooling of sovereignty. Not joining would damage our economy and reduce our influence. As with later projects, many believed it would have been better had the plan not been drafted; but it would not go away and it had to be dealt with.

Monnet and Schuman ensured that potential participants could enter the negotiations only once they accepted the principle of a High Authority. The Foreign Office advised this meant Britain 'could not easily retrace its steps if it disliked the effects' because it was 'likely to involve us in Europe beyond the point of no return'.[7] Not wishing to be seen to stifle such an imaginative attempt to end the historic conflict between France and Germany, Britain settled on the hope that the plan would never get off the drawing board. Oliver

Harvey, Ambassador to Paris, predicted that 'unless Britain comes in, the scheme cannot succeed'.[8]

Contrary to wishful thinking in Whitehall, France and West Germany were joined by Italy and the Benelux countries to form the European Coal and Steel Community, which came into being with Monnet at its head in August 1952. Unwilling to enter it, but unable to ignore it, Britain later acquired associate status without voting rights.

### The Messina Conference

The Six in the ECSC met at Messina in Sicily in June 1955 to discuss the formation of a Common Market. The Messina Conference set up a committee chaired by Paul-Henri Spaak, the Belgian Foreign Minister, which drafted proposals for common trade tariffs between the members and a united customs barrier to the rest of the world; for improved transport systems and better power supplies across their national borders; for the possible harmonisation of their social standards and monetary policy; and for supranational agencies including a court, commission, council of ministers and parliamentary assembly.

The Six invited Britain to attend Messina, this time without preconditions. Once again, Britain was paralysed by a move it did not want but could not disregard. Anthony Eden, the Prime Minister and a convinced Imperialist and Atlanticist, feared that the proposed supranational bodies would undermine British sovereignty. Once again, Britain simply hoped that the Six would never make their plan work. Gladwyn Jebb, Ambassador to Paris, forecast that 'no very spectacular developments are to be expected as a result of the Messina conference'.[9]

In a move calculated to keep an eye on those developments while maintaining a distance from them, Eden chose not to send a Cabinet Minister to Messina but instead to send a civil servant as an observer and as an insult. Russell Bretherton, who joined the Spaak committee, quickly realised the significance of the process and consequently appreciated Britain's timeless quandary. 'If we take an active part in trying to guide the final propositions, it will be difficult to avoid later on the presumption that we are, in some sense, committed to the result,' he wrote in a telegram to the Foreign Office that echoed the official line over the Schuman Plan. But, he prophetically added, 'if we sit back and say nothing, it's pretty certain that many more things will get into the report which would be unpleasant from the UK point of view whether we in the end took part in the Common Market or not'.[10]

Spaak noted that during the course of his committee's deliberations, 'the British attitude changed from one of mildly disdainful scepticism to growing fear' while Bretherton rarely spoke except 'to express doubt as to whether his country could accept whatever idea looked like becoming the basis of agreement at any given time'.[11] This, of course, was his brief. Yet the Foreign Office began to acknowledge the danger that the Six '*might* go ahead without us, and they *might* pull it off,' so officials concluded it would 'on balance be to the real and ultimate interest of the UK that the Common Market should collapse, with the result that there would be no need for the UK to face the embarrassing choice of joining it or abstaining from joining it'.[12] Having lurched between indifference and belligerence, Bretherton was instructed to withdraw in November 1955, which he did supposedly with the peroration 'Gentlemen, you are trying to negotiate something you will never be able to negotiate.

But if negotiated, it will not be ratified. And if ratified, it will not work.'[13] The Treaty of Rome was duly signed in March 1957, bringing about the European Economic Community in January 1958.

### Applications and vetoes

As these negotiations reached their denouement, Britain attempted a series of increasingly vainglorious wrecking measures that were too little too late. In July 1956 Britain fell back on plans for a Free Trade Area. The FTA was intended to envelop a wide membership, taking in the Six as well as those in the Organisation for European Economic Co-operation that Britain established in 1948 to oversee the implementation of the Marshall Plan and still chaired, but to focus a narrow ambition, promoting free trade within its own borders rather than acting as a single trading bloc. The aim was to supplant the supranational Common Market with an intergovernmental arrangement that had no political implications, no agricultural dimensions and no impact on Britain's preferential deals with the Commonwealth. Some have dreamed of the FTA ever since; now they even claim this is the kind of Europe they thought we finally joined in 1973. But although West Germany was tentatively receptive, it was rejected by France more than forty years ago.

In May 1960 Britain was forced to introduce a weakened European Free Trade Association of Seven, with Austria, Denmark, Norway, Portugal, Sweden and Switzerland. Britain's worst fears had been realised. Unable to impede the EEC, unable to dilute it, unable to rival it and unwilling to join it, Britain watched helplessly from the sidelines. Yet the impact of the Community on our domestic economy and our global standing made it the central subject of debate in

the country and it was inevitable that honest pragmatists
would soon conclude that the least-worst option was to join.
Harold Macmillan, the Prime Minister, announced the move
in July 1961, just over twelve months after the launch of the
EFTA and only four years after the Treaty of Rome had been
signed.

In a pamphlet published by the Conservative Party to
explain his decision, Macmillan confronted the traditional
fear of Europe. 'In the past, as a great maritime Empire, we
might give way to insular feelings of superiority over foreign
breeds and suspicion of our neighbours across the Channel,'
he admitted. But 'we have to consider the state of the world
as it is today and will be tomorrow, and not in outdated
terms of a vanished past' and 'this is no time to bury our
heads in the sands of the past and take the kind of parochial
view which regards Europe with distrust and suspicion'.
He also addressed the vexed question of sovereignty. 'In
renouncing some of our own sovereignty we would receive
in return a share of the sovereignty renounced by other
members,' he wrote.[14]

Macmillan's efforts were in vain. Charles de Gaulle, the
French President, seized on the Nassau agreement on
Polaris, concluded in December 1962, as the excuse he
needed to allege that Britain was committed more to the
United States than to Europe. The following month he
vetoed the application.

This devastating blow indicated just how far and how fast
we had fallen. The malaise was caught by Con O'Neill, the
senior British official in Brussels, in a note to Harold Wilson,
the incoming Prime Minister, that read like a stock-take of
Henry Tizard's terrible warning of two decades before. 'For
the last 20 years,' he wrote, 'this country has been adrift. On

the whole, it has been a period of decline in our international standing and power. This has helped to produce a national mood of frustration and uncertainty. We do not know where we are going and have begun to lose confidence in ourselves. Perhaps a point has now been reached when the acceptance of a new goal and a new commitment could give the country as a whole a focus around which to crystallise its hopes and energies. Entry into Europe might provide the stimulus and the target we require.'[15]

Wilson announced a second application. Yet this too ran into the buffers. Britain was forced to devalue the pound on 18 November 1967, and four days later de Gaulle declared that British interests – namely, the state of sterling, the commitment to the Commonwealth and the special relationship with the US – were incompatible with the Common Market. He wielded the French veto again. Having vacillated for so long, Britain was now in purgatory. The country's ambitions were in the hands of the ancient enemy.

### Entry

It was not until Charles de Gaulle was replaced by Georges Pompidou in 1969 that we regained a semblance of control over our own destiny. Edward Heath reopened talks about entry within days of taking office in 1970, in what was effectively Britain's third and by now desperate application. A White Paper offered a stark appraisal of the reasons for joining. 'During the 1950s the transformation of our position in the world was increasingly borne upon us,' it admitted, 'in terms of recurring economic problems at home and in the balance of payments, of the quickening move to independence among former colonies, and of a sense of diminishing influence in world counsels.'[16]

This cold realism was not borne upon everyone, however. Parliament considered the European Communities Bill for more than 300 hours, the longest debate since the war, and in the crucial vote on 28 October 1971 Heath's natural majority of 30 was threatened. Enoch Powell marshalled 40 Conservative rebels to join Labour's official opposition. A majority in favour of 112 was ensured only because in defiance of a three-line whip Roy Jenkins led 69 Labour MPs to vote for and a further 20 to abstain.

On 1 January 1973 Britain finally joined the EEC, 22 years after turning our backs on the ECSC. Many who supported entry then but have since changed their minds now claim they were misled, alleging they were assured the Community was nothing more than a free trade area. Yet this excuse of the zealot converts will not wash. Those who chose to ignore the evidence can blame no one but themselves.

The Government's White Paper asserted that 'the Six have firmly and repeatedly made clear that they reject the concept that European unity should be limited to the formation of a free trade area'.[17] That is why Britain was obliged to leave the intergovernmental EFTA in order to join the supranational EEC, which already had at its heart a Common Agricultural Policy that could never be described as an instrument of free trade.

Britain joined a Community that was already publicly committed to a single currency. The White Paper pointed to the 'clear intention' to 'progress towards economic and monetary union'. The Six had decided in The Hague in December 1969 to implement the recommendations of the Werner Report to achieve a single currency and the Nine – including the three applicant countries, Britain, Denmark and Ireland – affirmed that objective in Paris in October 1972.

And there was never any doubt about the implications of pooling sovereignty 'to lay the foundations of an ever closer union', words embedded at the beginning of the Treaty of Rome. At the conclusion of the Commons debate in October 1971, Heath, whose courage finally overcame the old fears of Europe, correctly remarked that 'I cannot over-emphasise tonight the importance of the vote which is being taken, the importance of the issue, the scale and quality of the decision and the impact that it will have equally inside and outside Britain.'[18]

## Britain in Europe, 1973–97

British leaders had crossed the threshold. They started using our membership of the European Economic Community as an instrument of government, although they failed to establish an enduring consensus for it among the public. Opposition parties have frequently been afflicted by spasms of anti-European populism, but no government has put its fears of Europe before our national interests. In fact, no government for more than forty years has been elected on an anti-European programme. Labour rejected entry in 1961 but proposed it in 1967; they officially voted against joining in 1971 but they effectively supported the Yes campaign in the 1975 referendum; Labour called for withdrawal in the early 1980s but back in government they have positively engaged since 1997. The Conservatives may have grown increasingly hostile to Europe since the end of the 1980s, but Tory leaders have made all the key moves towards integration: the decision to apply was taken by Harold Macmillan, accession was implemented under Edward Heath, the

THE FEAR OF EUROPE

Single European Act brought about by Margaret Thatcher and the Maastricht Treaty agreed by John Major. Yet none of them has consistently explained to voters the importance of Europe to Britain.

After 1973 Britain persisted in ignoring the unpalatable truths about our declining standing in the world, even as our economy plunged into an unprecedented era of stagflation and three-day weeks. That is why we have failed to carve out a leadership role on the Continent, instead continuing to fear all steps forward as a threat to our national identity, to be sternly resisted or adulterated, only to be feebly conceded later on.

### Referendum

Just fourteen months after joining, Britain opened talks that lasted for another fifteen months on whether to stay in. A new deal was negotiated and put to the people in the first national referendum in British history. It was a half-hearted beginning to our membership.

Tony Benn campaigned for a referendum primarily because the opinion polls suggested the anti-Marketeers would win. Harold Wilson conceded one principally because he saw no other way of healing the internal splits in the Labour Party. In March 1975 the Cabinet agreed to hold a referendum and to recommend a Yes vote, but to allow ministers including Benn, Barbara Castle, Michael Foot and Peter Shore to argue for a No vote. At the start of April the Yes vote was endorsed by Parliament, although a majority of junior ministers and Labour MPs voted against. At the end of April a special Labour Party Conference opted by two to one to favour withdrawal. Wilson was therefore in the absurd position of proposing to the country a deal which most of his

Government opposed and it was official Labour Party policy to reject.

The No campaign was a bizarre alliance led by Benn, Enoch Powell and Ian Paisley, and supported by the far left and the far right. Their central message was clear from their official statement, which alleged that the EEC 'sets out by stages to merge Britain with France, Germany, Italy and other countries into a single nation. This will take away from us the right to rule ourselves which we have enjoyed for centuries'.[19]

The Yes campaign, called 'Britain in Europe', directly addressed questions of pooled sovereignty and national identity. 'Our trade, our jobs, our food, our defence cannot be wholly within our own control,' its official statement said, 'that is why so much of the argument about *sovereignty* is a false one. It's not a matter of dry legal theory. The real test is how we can protect our own interests and exercise British influence in the world. The best way is to work with our friends and neighbours. If we came out, the Community would go on taking decisions which affect us vitally – but we would have no say in them. *We would be clinging to the shadow of British sovereignty while its substance flies out of the window.* The European Community does not pretend that each member nation is not different. It strikes a balance between the wish to express our own national personalities and the need for common action.'[20]

This case was best made during the campaign by none other than Margaret Thatcher. Of the suggestion that Britain should establish a free trade area and negotiate special access to the Common Market she noted 'the choice is whether to be outside the Community and yet have to accept everything which it decides' or 'whether to stay in the Community and have an influence over all those decisions which will seriously and closely affect the whole of our industrial life'. About the sanctity of national identity she observed that European integration permits 'the need to identify with one's own nation and country and the need to work together as a community and an alliance of nations for the well-being and betterment of mankind'. She concluded with the classic pro-Britain, pro-Europe message that today applies more than ever, 'I believe that Britain has always played a major role in the world and still has a major role to play. I do not believe it can play that role to best advantage on its own.'[21]

Although the issue had vexed the Westminster village for three decades, making and breaking political careers, it had little salience with the public until the moment they had the right to cast their vote. Years of apathy, confusion and hostility were quickly turned into popular support during the brief campaign. When Wilson announced the referendum in January, one Gallup poll typically showed just 33 per cent were for 'In' and 41 per cent were for 'Out'. On 5 June, with a high turnout of 64.5 per cent, to the question 'do you think that the United Kingdom should stay in the European Community?' 17,379,000 (67.2 per cent) voted Yes and 8,470,000 (32.8 per cent) voted No. It was a clear majority, greater than any government has received in a general election, of more than two to one.

The victorious pro-Europeans believed that the referendum had finally settled Britain's relations with Europe once and for all. Benn conceded when he heard the result that 'by an overwhelming majority the British people have voted to stay in and I am sure that everybody would want to accept that'.[22] In fact, it was merely the signal for the anti-Marketeers to regroup and redouble their efforts.

### The Single European Act

As the debate about Europe raged in the Conservative Party throughout the 1980s and 1990s, its supporters have been confronted with an incontrovertible fact: every single one of its leaders in government since Harold Macmillan has found no practical alternative to furthering British national interests through Europe. There is no doubt that Margaret Thatcher was never as keen as Michael Heseltine, her nemesis, but he perfectly explained her plight. 'No one pretends that Mrs Thatcher liked the process,' he said, 'but that makes the case stronger. If there had been a practical alternative,' he added, 'be sure that Mrs Thatcher would have found it and argued for it.'[23] In office, she did not.

After 1958 the Common Market overhauled tariffs, but almost thirty years later a mountain of regulations remained a barrier to free trade. In 1985 Thatcher encouraged Arthur Cockfield, one of Britain's Commissioners, to identify 300 rules to be harmonised or removed by 1992, freeing the movement of goods and services, people and capital, to create a Single Market. Simultaneously, Jacques Delors, the President of the Commission, unveiled plans to extend hugely the process of Qualified Majority Voting – which allocates votes to each country roughly according to its size, and allows a majority of about 70 per cent of those votes to pass legislation binding on all members – in order to smooth the decision-making process and so allow the Single Market to function.

Thatcher was confronted by a dilemma: she could not reduce the power of protectionism in Europe without also limiting the reach of the British veto. She endorsed both Cockfield's and Delors's proposals. The resulting Single European Act was then lauded as 'Thatcherism on a European scale', even though it also committed the European Community, as it became known, to the 'progressive realisation of economic and monetary union'.

Michael Butler, the senior British official during these negotiations, reports that he watched 'her reason overcoming her prejudices'.[24] But it was the last time she was prepared to compromise to get her way. In fact, Downing Street insisted that the word 'compromise' was never again to be mentioned by officials in their briefs to her. Her attitude became boorish as she adopted a winner-takes-all approach, which hardened media and public opinion but ended up as self-defeating because in her dealings with European leaders she lost far more than she won. It was forgotten that in negotiations outcome not input is the best measure of success.

In this frame of mind, Thatcher dug in against monetary cooperation to complete the Single Market, first by avoiding membership of the Exchange Rate Mechanism, then by opposing the fledgling single currency. She had condemned Callaghan's decision not to join the ERM in 1978 as a sad day because Britain was 'openly classified among the poorest and least influential members' of the Community.[25] But she resisted pressure from Nigel Lawson, the Chancellor, and Geoffrey Howe, the Foreign Secretary, to join in 1985, largely because she felt it would be an admission that her Government could not run its own anti-inflation policy successfully.

The turning point came in 1988. This was when Britain began exporting more to the EC than to the rest of the world, when Delors was appointed to chair a committee of central bank governors to examine the feasibility of introducing a single currency, and when he was rapturously received by the TUC Conference for his emphasis on the social dimension. Thatcher's prejudices overwhelmed her reason. In a twisted reverse of Clausewitz's famous dictum, she seemed to believe that in the Community politics is the continuation of war by other means.

Thatcher then delivered what is tragically the most famous speech on Europe ever made by a sitting British prime minister. 'We have not successfully rolled back the frontiers of the state in Britain only to see them reimposed at a European level, with a European superstate exercising a new dominance from Brussels,' she raged in Bruges. She attacked 'Brussels bureaucrats' for what she saw as their socialist subversion of Britishness, thus opening the flood-gates to the Euro-sceptics, a term that suddenly entered common usage.

The temperature of the debate soared. In 1990 Nicholas Ridley was forced to resign from the Cabinet for complain-ing in *The Spectator* about what he called 'a German racket designed to take over the whole of Europe'. He lamented that 'this rushed takeover by the Germans on the worst possible basis, with the French behaving like poodles to the Germans, is absolutely intolerable'.[26] At the same time, *The Independent on Sunday* printed surreal details of a confidential meeting that Thatcher had convened at Chequers to consider 'What does history tell us about the character and behaviour of the German-speaking people of Europe?' and 'Is it better psychologically to "stand up to Germany" or to pursue a friendly approach?' According to the leaked minutes, the gathering believed that 'angst, aggressiveness, assertiveness, bullying, egotism, inferiority complex, sentimentality' were all 'an abiding part of the German character' and 'the way in which the Germans currently used their elbows and threw their weight about in the European Community suggested that a lot had still not changed' in fifty years.[27]

This was the bizarre backdrop against which Thatcher's curtain finally fell. The cue came from the publication of the Delors Report in April 1989, which outlined a three-stage timetable to Economic and Monetary Union, obliging all EC countries to join the ERM at Stage One. In the perennial predicament, Britain could choose either to sign up and influence the process, or to opt out and stand aside as an observer.

Thatcher was bounced into announcing her intention to enter the ERM by Lawson and Howe in June 1989. In revenge, she effectively forced Lawson to resign and Howe was demoted. The new Chancellor, John Major, resorted to the antique tactic: he launched a rival, weaker scheme, the so-called 'hard ecu', that could, should or would – depending on the audience – lead to a single currency. The new Foreign Secretary, Douglas Hurd, restated the ancient problem: Britain must not be 'prickly, defensive or negative' but must engage positively with our partners lest 'we isolate ourselves by shutting ourselves off, raising the drawbridge of argument, acting as if we were a beleaguered island'.[28]

An all-too-familiar sequence of events unfolded. Thatcher predicted the Delors Report would prove unpopular and unworkable, and she called for delays to its ambitious timetable. But the 'hard ecu' garnered no sympathy, so she was ultimately forced to take Britain into the ERM in October 1990. After the Delors Report was accepted a few weeks later, she boiled her lexicon about the single currency down to a single repetitive syllable: 'No. No. No.'[29]

Within a fortnight Geoffrey Howe was gone. His resignation speech was not just a damning indictment of Thatcher's attitude to Europe, but a devastating verdict on Britain's entire post-war relationship with the Continent. We often seemed 'to look out upon a continent that is positively teeming with ill-intentioned people, scheming,' causing us 'to retreat into a ghetto of sentimentality about our past and so diminish our own control over our own destiny in the future,' he chided. 'We must at all costs avoid presenting ourselves yet again with an oversimplified choice, a false antithesis, a bogus dilemma, between one alternative, starkly labelled "cooperation between independent sovereign states" and a second, equally crudely labelled alternative, "centralised, federal superstate", as if there were no middle way,' he advised. In what should have been a coda to this sorry story, he reflected, 'we have paid heavily in the past for late starts and squandered opportunities in Europe. We dare not let that happen again.'[30]

### The Maastricht Treaty

John Major had not so much as visited the United States before he became Foreign Secretary, but as Prime Minister he signalled a much less insular approach. 'My aims for Britain in the Community can be simply stated,' he famously asserted, 'I want us to be where we belong. At the *very* heart of Europe. Working with our partners in building the future.' And he approached the eternal puzzle with a fresh attitude. 'Europe is made up of nation-states: their vitality and diversity are sources of strength,' he argued, 'the important thing is to strike the right balance between closer cooperation and a proper respect for national institutions and traditions.'[31]

Major caught the essence of the pro-Britain, pro-Europe case. But his time in office was poisoned by a clash between the real world he lived and breathed – where most aspects of domestic policy increasingly had a foreign policy dimension and where Britain's national interests depended on everyday negotiations in Europe – and the fantasy world that a few flat-earthers in his party wished existed. He was held hostage by a handful of backbenchers as his wafer-thin majority ebbed away.

The Maastricht Treaty, concluded in December 1991, consummated the Delors Report by conceiving mechanisms for Economic and Monetary Union, a single currency and a European Central Bank, to be born by 1999. The history of Britain's approach to these occasions was by now sufficiently legendary that during the negotiations the President of the Commission advised Douglas Hurd not to follow the example of Russell Bretherton at Messina in refusing to participate in a European venture in the hope that it would fail.[32]

Major negotiated opt-outs from both the single currency and the Social Chapter – hailed as 'game, set and match' to Britain – and after the general election he embarked on the laborious labyrinth of Commons approval. Just 22 Tory rebels voted against the Bill at the first opportunity in May 1992, but in the next four months two events became inextricably tangled into the sovereign Parliament's deliberations about the single currency and consequently paralysed the Government.

On 2 June 50.7 per cent of those voting in a Danish referendum refused to endorse Maastricht – a majority of just 48,000 – leaving it in limbo as it required ratification by all its signatories to become law; 69 Euro-sceptics immediately signed a motion calling for a 'fresh start' to scrap the Treaty. Then on 16 September sterling crashed through its ERM floor of DM2.95; the pound dropped below DM2.35 within weeks, a devaluation of more than 15 per cent. The Euro-sceptics seized on what became known as Black Wednesday, the moment that Britain was ejected from the ERM, to wrongly conflate this humiliation with the Maastricht proposals for a single currency.

Lobby groups multiplied and by the time the legislative upheaval climaxed in a vote of confidence in July 1993, after the Danes had reversed their decision, almost thirty organisations were dedicated to dislocating Britain's place at the heart of Europe and therefore destroying Major's foreign and economic policies. In Westminster William Cash suddenly shot to prominence as he set new records for disloyalty, tabling 240 amendments and voting 47 times against his own Government on three-line whips in just thirteen months. In Cabinet a faction including Peter Lilley, Michael Portillo and John Redwood let it be known that they were against Maastricht. In an unguarded moment before a live microphone, Major allowed his frustration to show by accusing his party of 'harking back to the golden age that never was and is now invented,' and branding the Cabinet trio and former ministers, apparently including Thatcher, 'the bastards'.[33]

The aim of all this Euro-sceptic hyperactivity was to subject Maastricht to a veto or a referendum. They did not just want to stop Britain from joining, they wanted to prevent the single currency from coming about. They knew then what they now deny, that once it existed the economic conditions would be transformed and Britain would be affected whether we were in it or not. Major resisted. After all, he had negotiated the deal, Thatcher had never vetoed a European initiative and she had previously denounced the idea of referendums.

The Euro-sceptics focused their attack not on the economics of the single currency, but on the question of national sovereignty. Bile spewed from a flood of books and pamphlets. In his own tract – typically subtitled *The Battle for Britain* – Cash came close to calling the Community 'fascist', warning darkly that Germany's 'previous bids for power have been made in the name of Europe'.[34]

While it was evident they were prepared to fight in the last ditch against Maastricht, it also became apparent that the Euro-sceptics had no alternative but shouting No. Tory MP Michael Spicer made a series of demands in his snap book *A Treaty Too Far* that included an Act of Parliament to identify a list of matters that the European Union as it was now called should never be allowed to affect, an Act to guarantee the supremacy of Parliament over the EU, and fundamental renegotiation of the Treaty of Rome to turn Europe into the much-vaunted but long-rejected free trade area. But he had no plan B if this agenda was unacceptable to our Continental partners, as it inevitably would have been.[35]

The first significant figure to admit where the logic of this argument headed was Norman Lamont, bitter from his sacking as Chancellor after the ERM fiasco. In balancing the pros and cons of continued membership of the EU, he told a fringe meeting at the 1994 Conservative Party Conference that he might accept Britain in an 'outer tier' that 'involved only the free trade parts'. But he did not think this would be amenable to the inner tier, as it would not amount to a 'two-speed Europe' because there were 'two completely different directions' where 'Britain is on a collision course with her partners'. Hence, he tentatively suggested, 'it may mean contemplating withdrawal'.[36]

## Anti-Europeanism today

The Maastricht Treaty cleaved a new fault line in the debate about Europe in Britain, between those prepared for further engagement in the right conditions and those refusing to countenance involvement regardless of the circumstances. This was the moment when Euro-scepticism became a misnomer as many active Euro-sceptics turned into out-and-out anti-Europeans.

Despite Britain's opt-out, Maastricht initiated the very real prospect that we might one day join the single currency. After 1996 when John Major, followed a few months later by the new Labour leader Tony Blair, announced that Britain would not opt in without a referendum, the argument spread beyond Westminster to the country. Since then, public bemusement has edged towards genuine scepticism as the debate has become skewed and irrational. While voters are bombarded with a daily diet of myths and scares about Europe in the press, and lobby groups and fringe figures have captured space in the public debate for their alternatives, it is sometimes difficult for the sensible pro-Britain, pro-Europe case to get a reasonable hearing.

### Straight bananas

If we were to believe what we read in the newspapers then among the choice items currently banned under 'Eurocrat' decree are bent bananas, curved cucumbers and apples less than 55 millimetres across. Other traditional British delights that have supposedly been outlawed include mushy peas, the sale of shandy in pints and the smacking of children by their parents.

In tabloid lore, harmonisation means making British things foreign. In what we are repeatedly told is Brussels's drive to harmonise everything, just a smattering of the improbable victims identified by the press are the temperature at which whelks are stored, summer holidays and the MOT car test.

Less discerning readers may believe that thanks to the staple of trumped-up European Union diktats to which they are treated, Cornish clotted cream is now made in Brittany, brandy butter has been renamed 'spreadable fat' and information about possible allergies in nuts is written on the packaging in Latin not English. They may even think that Britain has been forced to adopt French-style squat toilets, or that our kettles take longer to boil because the EU has slashed the electric voltage into our homes.[37]

These are just a few of the fabrications and distortions that have soaked into our national consciousness, sadly proving wrong the catchphrase of *The Sun* columnist Richard Littlejohn, 'they couldn't make it up'. They can, and do, almost every day. Their motive is to create the impression that the EU is by stealth building the much-feared though imaginary 'superstate' devoted to destroying our traditional way of life.[38] As *The Sun* summarised this caricature, the EU is trying to 'CASTRATE parliament, SHACKLE our courts and hand TOTAL POLITICAL CONTROL to Brussels'.[39] Yet when this version of events is challenged, the media becomes especially high-handed. With no irony intended, *The Sun* later fumed, 'there are even hints the EU might use obscure laws against blasphemy to gag the Press if it dares to criticise Brussels in future'.[40]

A recent academic survey of press attitudes to Europe – tellingly titled *Insulting the Public* – concluded that much reporting stems from 'the most inadmissible distortion and xenophobia' and a 'predominantly crude stereotyping of peoples, distortion of issues and omission of information which would be laughable were not the issues at stake so important'.[41]

Value judgements have infected newspapers not just in editorials but also in news reports. There are undoubted commercial pressures, because scare stories with verisimilitude write copy and sell papers better than the mundane realities of life, but in extreme cases these agendas are driven by political ideology. Conrad Black, the Canadian proprietor of *The Daily Telegraph* and *The Sunday Telegraph*, has shamelessly run a personal campaign through his organs for Britain to join the North American Free Trade Agreement. 'Britain should quit the EU and link up instead with the United States and Canada in a free trade area which would eclipse the influence of Brussels,' he said.[42] And at the height of Tony Blair's popularity, *The Sun* labelled him 'The Most Dangerous Man in Britain' just because he refused to rule out the option of entering the single currency.[43]

By contrast, the less antagonistic press tends not to shout nearly so loudly for their corner, and some spend almost as much time criticising the tactics of the pro-Europeans as the principles of the antis. Like the broadcasters, they do not devote anything like the priority to European issues that their rivals do. During 2000 a Europe story appeared on the front page of *The Sun* seven times more often than in *The Mirror*. For television and radio news and the pro-European press, Europe usually becomes a big story only when it impinges on domestic politics, through conflict between political parties and real or imagined splits within parties. All of this has rendered public debate about the most important and complex topic, whether or not we should join the euro, totally unbalanced.

### The pressure for withdrawal

Under cover of this welter of hostility from the press, anti-Europeans have become recklessly assertive, strongly organised and heavily funded by wealthy fanatics. James Goldsmith claimed to have invested £20 million in his Referendum Party, which in the 1997 election contested every parliamentary constituency where the main candidates refused to advocate a plebiscite on further European integration. It polled a miserly 811,849 votes across 547 seats, at the princely sum of £24.68 per vote. This 2.6 per cent share of the total was still higher than that of its rival, the UK Independence Party, which argues for outright withdrawal: it achieved just 0.3 per cent of the vote.

Paul Sykes, who is reputedly worth about £400 million, boasted that he spent more than £2 million in 1997 promoting the 317 Conservative candidates – including over half of the 164 elected – who agreed to write in their personal election addresses that they would never vote for the euro, regardless of the circumstances. As well as owning the British Democracy Campaign, he also set up the Democracy Movement, which received money from Annabel Goldsmith to target literature against 160 pro-European MPs in 2001; yet it failed to unseat a single one of them. Sykes channelled his own funds through the UK Independence Party in 2001, bragging that he spent over £100,000 a day to support his view that 'it is no longer possible to remain members of the EU and at the same time retain British self-government'.[44] Despite paying for newspaper and poster advertisements as well as leaflets that were sent to 20 million households, his money enabled UKIP to inspire only a dismal 1.5 per cent of voters.

Although the activities of these fringe parties and lobby groups may have cost the Conservatives no more than a handful of seats in 1997 and 2001, they certainly helped drag many of its candidates to attack 'Brussels' in an effort to appease the vehement anti-Europeans. And no doubt money from Sykes and the Goldsmith family will be made available to No campaigners for any referendum on the single currency.

The link between the Tory Party and No campaigners is symbolised by Stuart Wheeler. He gave £5 million to the Conservative Party just before the election, warning that 'if Kenneth Clarke was to become leader after the election, I do not see myself supporting the Conservatives or any other party led by somebody who is so keen to go into the euro'.[45] In fact, he reportedly decided to transfer his largesse to the anti-euro lobby Business for Sterling, of which he is a leading member.

With backing like this, fearmongering anti-European lobby groups have spread like a plague in the past decade; there are up to fifty at the latest count, a far cry from the days when the Anti-Common Market League fought alone in 1961. Each has a minuscule membership and the same faces crop up again and again at the top of them all. Richard Body – who resigned the Tory whip over Maastricht, sparking John Major to remark 'whenever I hear the name Richard Body, I hear the sound of white coats flapping' – is president of the ACML. Its quarterly bulletin recently declared 'we have always been closely connected with the Conservative Party. We worked not unsuccessfully to support those candidates and MPs who are anti-Market, to influence further those who are Euro-sceptic if not yet fully opposed to British membership of the Common Market.'[46] Body is also president of the Campaign for an Independent Britain, which advocates withdrawal, and vice-president of Conservatives Against a Federal Europe.

CAFE demands new terms of membership or 'if it is not possible to attain these ends by negotiation, we must withdraw from the European Union'.[47] It was launched in 1996 by Body and the eight other whipless rebels; during the 1997 Parliament it attracted nineteen members of the Conservative frontbench team and almost a third of Tory MPs; since the 2001 election its ranks have swelled even further. Another vice-president is Tim Bell, chair of the Conservative Party's Keep The Pound campaign. Another is Teddy Taylor, who set up the Conservative European Reform Group. Another is William Cash, who established the European Foundation. Yet another is Michael Spicer, chair of both the European Research Group and the Congress for Democracy, one of the many embryonic No campaigns for any referendum on the single currency.

The supposedly acceptable putative No campaign is that run by Business for Sterling and New Europe, which claim to be anti-euro but pro-EU. Yet while virtually none of their literature ever stresses the benefits of Europe, many of their leading personnel have close links with anti-EU organisations. As long ago as 1994 Rodney Leach, chair of BfS, called for 'an accurate cost-benefit analysis of withdrawal' because 'Europe has become a net negative factor'.[48] More than a dozen members of its ruling council also help run the Bruges Group, which was formed in 1989 to 'campaign for a Europe less subject to centralised control than that emerging in Brussels'; but a decade later it too demands new terms of membership or 'in the event that such a renegotiation is unobtainable, the Bruges Group advocates withdrawal from the European Union'.[49] Several of the founder signatories of BfS have stood as candidates for the Referendum Party and lots are office holders of CAFE or other bodies committed to renegotiation or withdrawal.

Many of these lobby groups are brought together with the Campaign Against Euro-Federalism, the Campaign for United Kingdom Conservatism and the main left-wing group the Labour Euro-Safeguards Campaign, to name but a few, in the intricate web of the Anti-Maastricht Alliance. Others in the melting pot that want Britain out of Europe include the British National Party, Norris McWhirter's Freedom Association, the Communist Party and Arthur Scargill's Socialist Labour Party.

### There Is No Alternative

Unsurprisingly, this maze of lobbying pressure has altered the centre of gravity within the Conservative Party. Just eighteen months after the 1997 landslide defeat and even before the single currency had been launched, John Major's compromise of 'wait and see' to the euro was formally abandoned. Instead members endorsed William Hague's policy to oppose it, in all circumstances, until at least after the following parliament, then up to ten years away. That ballot ended the divisions that had bedevilled Tory strategists since Margaret Thatcher's demise because the pro-Europeans were routed. Consequently, the policy became clearer and the attitude harder, but many big beasts from the Thatcher and Major Cabinets – including Leon Brittan, Kenneth Clarke, Michael Heseltine, Geoffrey Howe and Chris Patten – were left at odds with their party in public for the first time. And it was a red rag to the bullish anti-Europeans to press for even greater hostility.

Conservative anti-Europeans have learned from their Labour counterparts, the Bennites of twenty years before, how to make transitional demands that drag their party towards more extreme positions. This trend was spotted in

1999 by *The Times* columnist and former Tory MP Matthew Parris. 'The anti-Europeans' strategy is now clear, and shrewd it is,' he wrote, 'they intend to bounce the party in a series of little sideways moves whose ultimate objective is head-on confrontation between Britain and her European partners. By then the stakes will be raised so high that, bounced into a corner, Britain must threaten to quit. Then we quit.'[50] John Major noticed it too. 'There are some people in the Conservative Party who have been pushing the ratchet for years,' he said, 'they are pushing and pushing and I believe trying to create a circumstance in which there will then one day be no choice but to decide whether we stay in or leave.'[51]

Immediately after the 1997 election they pushed harder. Rather than standing up to them as Major had done, Hague tilted towards them. Looking for votes during the leadership contest, he declared in William Cash's *European Journal* that 'I am opposed to the single currency in principle'.[52] His later policy for public consumption did not quite say 'never', but by setting an arbitrary date it was hard to believe he would ever be in favour of joining, even if it proved to be in our national interests. John Redwood, a vice-president of CAFE, detected the contradiction, remarking 'it's like saying we're against rape for ten years'.[53]

Michael Portillo and Iain Duncan Smith have pushed the ratchet further, effectively ruling out the euro for good. 'As long as we are outside the single currency we will be very influential,' said Portillo, 'because we will be an example of how a country performs whose currency and interest rates meet its own economic conditions. That is how we would retain influence, but only – of course – if people believe we are serious and are going to stick to it.'[54] 'A Conservative Party led by me would be settled on the issue of Europe,' added Duncan Smith, a vice-president of CAFE, 'it should be no surprise to anyone that I am opposed to entry into the euro in principle'.[55]

During the 2001 election campaign, the floodgates were opened by Margaret Thatcher, who insisted 'I would *never* be prepared to give up our own currency'.[56] As many as 250 Tory PPCs publicly agreed. The pressure towards ruling out the option of joining for ever, rather than just for one parliament, even swept away Francis Maude, the Shadow Foreign Secretary in charge of the official policy, who felt obliged to say that 'we think it will never be right for Britain to join the single currency'.[57] Surrounded by ubiquitous 'Save the Pound' placards, Hague and Portillo declared the 2001 election a referendum on the euro and were decisively trounced. Yet if the Conservatives had won then people would have been denied a say in this crucial decision because they were opposed to holding a plebiscite.

Anti-Europeans are well aware that a No vote in a referendum would not be a return to the status quo ante; they hope it would be a staging post on the road to withdrawal. Two weeks before the Danish referendum in 2000, Margrethe Auken, a leading No campaigner, let the cat out of the bag when she switched to the Yes camp following a visit to Britain. 'It's clear that many of the Conservatives are totally against the EU,' she reported; 'for them, stopping the euro is the first step towards total withdrawal. That's something that could set off centrifugal forces in Europe and I think it's getting dangerous.'[58]

Beneath the darkening rhetoric against the single currency, some leading figures have shown the way to the exit. As early as 1996, Duncan Smith claimed that 'the public is ready to go for Britain repatriating its powers from the EU, which could eventually mean pulling out'.[59] During the 1999 Conservative conference Norman Tebbit declared that the party slogan – to be 'in Europe not run by Europe' – was virtually meaningless because 'we are ruled by Europe across great swaths of our life'.[60] Leaving was implicit in the bizarre comments made by Thatcher later the same day when she insisted that 'in my lifetime all our problems have come from mainland Europe and all the solutions have come from the English-speaking nations across the world who have kept law-abiding liberty alive for the future'.[61]

In the past few years leading Conservatives have embraced a series of policies that had been condemned out of hand when they were originally demanded by the Bennites in the 1980s and the Euro-sceptics in the 1990s. To start with they pledged to renegotiate the Treaty of Rome. Not only is renegotiation virtually impossible as it would mean unpicking the carefully crafted agreements of Britain and fourteen other sovereign nation-states dating back more than forty years, but the intention is impotent without the threat to withdraw. That is why both halves of this equation feature in the mission statements of CAFE and the Bruges Group. 'To force the pace in negotiations we may have to be prepared to contemplate withdrawal,' Maude has conceded.[62]

They promised to veto all future European treaties unless they contain a 'flexibility clause' allowing Britain to opt out of their provisions. Any treaty changes require the unanimous agreement of all fifteen members, and it is inconceivable the others would accept this demand. So the threat to wield the veto would either turn out to be an empty bluff or cut away Britain's standing in Europe.

They adopted the agenda outlined in Michael Spicer's 1992 book for an Act of Parliament identifying a list of 'reserve powers' that the European Union should never be allowed to affect and an Act to 'guarantee the supremacy of Parliament' over the EU. If ever implemented, as a unilateral declaration of independence these policies would probably be illegal under existing treaties and they would certainly destroy our influence on the Continent.

And they embraced Goldsmith's programme to hold a referendum before ratifying any new treaties. In the case of the Nice Treaty, concluded in 2000, which they pledged not to ratify but to renegotiate, this would have entailed delaying or abandoning altogether attempts to enlarge the membership of the Union, which has long been an agreed objective for all British political parties.

Although most anti-Europeans have stopped short of advocating outright withdrawal, sympathetic noises have been made about the possibility of joining the European Economic Area or the North American Free Trade Agreement. This is simply code for leaving the EU. Individual members cannot conclude unilateral trade agreements because the European Commission, guided by the Council of Ministers, conducts external trade relations on behalf of the whole Union; so to enter the EEA or NAFTA we would have to turn our back on the EU.

The fact of the matter is that anti-Europeans have been running out of options. Their rising hysteria against the single currency has emboldened them to make increasingly outrageous claims about the threat that the EU supposedly poses to Britain. No stopgap solutions, all of which are bound to be unacceptable to our partners, could possible address these imagined dangers. Though some are reluctant to follow their own logic, and others are happy to hide behind the veneer of expedient positions, many have edged towards openly accepting that they have no alternative to outright withdrawal. If Britain were to adopt that view, allowing the irrational Little England fear of Europe to outweigh the calculable benefits, it would overturn the lessons of fifty years of history and severely damage our national interests.

# The Benefits of Europe

## British prosperity

Until recently, most pro-Europeans believed that the 1975 referendum had finally stabilised Britain's relations with Europe. The result was decisive and we were in. 'Britain in Europe', the coalition that ran the Yes campaign, immediately disbanded and its leaders went back to their normal activity – in politics, business, the trade unions, the voluntary sector and elsewhere – assuming that Europe was now part of their natural working environment. For a quarter of a century almost nobody, with a few notable exceptions, felt any need to restate the case for our involvement because we all took the benefits for granted. Meanwhile, the anti-Marketeers regrouped and suspicious Euro-scepticism turned into venomous anti-Europeanism as a campaign developed to resist any further integration and even to unpick the 1975 settlement.

Adding incompetence to complacency, the European Union itself has been a terrible advocate of its own interests.

In fact, it has been a public relations disaster. Unlike governments – whose ministers regularly appear in the media to
justify how they are spending taxpayers' money and reveal
their strategies for improving education and health and so on
– the EU inevitably has no recognisable spokespeople to
explain what it is doing, not least because of the proper dominance of the member countries. Governments themselves
have often been of little help because they have tended to
take the credit for popular measures while blaming the European Commission for more controversial proposals, even
when they backed them in the Council of Ministers. With
few rival sources of digestible information, the press has
therefore been unusually powerful in shaping public opinions about complex European developments.

So it is little wonder that the pro-Britain, pro-Europe case
has not been heard. As alarmist attacks on the EU have intensified in the past decade, support has slumped: the nadir was
a BBC/ICM poll at the start of 2000 showing that one in
three favoured withdrawal.[1] At the same time, people pro-
claim themselves less well informed about European issues
than ever before: by the spring of 2001 up to 70 per cent
admitted they knew little about the EU.[2] It is to combat this
apparent rising hostility and ignorance that 'Britain in
Europe' was re-formed in 1999. And we have a good tale to
tell. Before joining, the pro-Marketeers made bold claims
about the economic advantages. Yet even those predictions
have been surpassed. We, as individuals and as a nation, are
quite simply much richer because of our membership.

### Trade

The European internal market – starting with the Common
Market, then the Single Market and now the single currency

– has been designed to foster free trade, generate wealth and create jobs. Britain is an island trading nation, which has been dependent on buying and selling abroad since the Industrial Revolution, and these days the equivalent of 26 per cent of our national income comes from foreign trade, compared to only 12 per cent for the United States and an average of 21 per cent for industrialised nations.[3] Therefore, the greater the stability in our relationships with our biggest trading partners, the more prosperous our economy will be. As our reliance on Commonwealth preferences has diminished while our ties to the United States are stronger politically than economically, our biggest trading partners are now in Europe.

Since 1973 the proportion of our goods exported to the Six founding members of the European Economic Community has virtually doubled from 21 per cent to 41 per cent, and the share sent to the European Union as a whole has leaped from 35 per cent to 57 per cent.[4] Before we joined, less than £5 billion of our trade was with the rest of Europe; today it is £132 billion, more than half our trade. Of this, £107 billion is in goods and £25 billion is in services. Eight of our top ten trading partners are in the EU.[5] And the EU is the leading export market for every single region and nation of the United Kingdom.[6]

This is both a phenomenal rate of increase and an extraordinary level of dependence. By comparison, we send only 16 per cent of our goods to the US and just 12 per cent to Asia. The value of our goods exported to the EU is more than four times higher than to the US, we sell twice as much to Belgium as to Japan and more to France than to the entire Commonwealth.

This trade has boosted all sectors of our economy, leaving

swathes of industry and commerce reliant on our links to
Europe. For example, in 2000 Britain produced almost 2 million motor vehicles, 70 per cent of which were exported, and
80 per cent of those went to EU countries. It is not just big
business that is bound in: up to 40 per cent of small and
medium-sized enterprises, 750,000 firms, are connected to
the EU, some directly but many dependent on supplying
larger companies that trade with Europe.

The bond between British exporters and European consumers has been cemented by the internal market. The
Common Market stimulated trade by removing tariffs and
duties. The Single Market created the single largest consumer
market in the world by abolishing or harmonising regulations, so freeing the movement of people and capital, goods
and services. Initiated in 1986, it enlarged our natural trading
area from 60 million British citizens to 370 million European
consumers. This unlocked opportunities to sell across the
Continent under a single set of standards without expensive
and time-consuming red tape: the scrapping of ten million
customs forms has saved British firms around £135 million a
year. And for consumers, increased competition has cut
prices: within Europe air fares and telephone charges have
halved since 1986. In its first five years, across the EU including in Britain, the Single Market created a million jobs,
helped reduce inflation by up to 1.5 per cent and boosted
GDP by about 1.5 per cent.[7]

The EU is the largest trading bloc in the world, accounting for around 40 per cent of the global total. As such, it has
advanced the interests of its members far better than any of
them could have done alone at international trade negotiations. With the combined clout of one large group, the fifteen have pushed for free trade agreements through the

World Trade Organisation, opening the markets of the Far East to products like Scotch whisky, for instance. Furthermore, multilateral treaties between the EU and the former colonies of its members, such as through the Lomé and Cotonou Conventions, have allowed Commonwealth countries in Africa, the Caribbean and the Pacific to access the internal market without confronting protective barriers.[8]

The value to Britain of being part of the EU trading region cannot be overstated. The lack of a level playing field up to 1973 seriously damaged our national interests by restricting our economic potential, as Margaret Thatcher noted in her memoirs. 'We had underrated the potential advantage to Britain of access to the Common Market,' she wrote of the urgent need to get in; 'neither the European Free Trade Association (EFTA) nor our links with the Commonwealth and the United States offered us the trading future we needed'.[9] She was right then and our ties are even stronger now.

### Inward investment

Freer global trade has encouraged multinational businesses to open factories across the world so that they can supply products to local consumers more efficiently. The flow of this inward investment, as it is known, totalled £535 billion in 1999 alone; more than one-third of that, £190 billion, came to the European Union. Companies from Asia and the United States started rapidly expanding into Europe in the mid-1980s when the Single Market was born. Inward investment shot into the EU, up from a stock worth £180 billion in 1985 to £1,000 billion by 1999.[10]

Britain has won the lion's share; it had accumulated £250 billion by 1999. Although we invest more in the rest of the

EU than other EU countries invest here, before the launch of
the euro we received 28 per cent of all inward investment
into Europe. We got 40 per cent of Japanese and 40 per cent
of US investment into the EU, more than goes to all of Asia
put together. There are now at least 1,000 Japanese and 2,500
US companies based here, many of which are household
names like Nissan and Ford that provide work for entire
communities. Inward investment has been key to the regeneration of regions like the North East, South Wales and Central Scotland that suffered from de-industrialisation and
appalling unemployment levels in the early 1980s.

Britain has been so successful at attracting foreign firms
largely because of our enterprise environment. But we
would not have won nearly so much were we not also part
of the EU. Our language, our flexible markets and our low
taxes offer the ideal home for business, but foreigners do not
come here just to sell to Britons: it is their bridgehead from
which to export across Europe. Inward investors export 75
per cent of their production, comprising 40 per cent of our
total exports. When we were locked out of Europe before
1973, our slice of inward investment shrank from 40 per cent
to 15 per cent, mirroring the relative decline of our economy. If we were to lack complete access to the internal
market now, inward investors have made it clear that they
would certainly consider leaving and relocating in other
member countries.

### Jobs
Up to 3.5 million British jobs, about one in nine British
workers, now depend on our trading relations with the
European Union, four times more than rely on our links
with the United States.[11] At least 2.7 million jobs are directly

connected through the production of goods and services exported to the EU; over a million of these are in manufacturing and half a million each are in the financial, retail and wholesale sectors. Inward investors employ up to one million Britons, around a quarter of manufacturing workers; and even though only 2 per cent of Britons work on the land, trade with the EU sustains agricultural employment for almost 150,000 people. In addition to these, a further 500,000 jobs are indirectly tied to the EU, either in domestic business for companies that largely depend on foreign trade for profits or as suppliers to those that export.[12]

Among the largest exporters, the EU accounts for almost half of the trade of British-owned firms and two-thirds of foreign-owned companies; from inward investors based in Britain but owned by parents outside Europe, exports to the EU compose three-quarters of their trade. 'It is these firms who would be most likely to move elsewhere if exports from the UK were to be subject to EU trade barriers,' argues the respected independent organisation the National Institute of Economic and Social Research; and at least some of these would inevitably be reimposed if we were to withdraw.[13]

In a comprehensive examination of the wider costs of leaving the EU, NIESR concluded that if trade barriers were reintroduced then they would raise the effective price of our exports by around 9 per cent. This would inevitably result in the relocation of so many foreign firms to other countries within the internal market that our stock of inward investment might be cut by up to one-third in manufacturing. In fact, when the likely impact of leaving was run through the NIESR economic model, it was calculated that after two decades the volume of our output would be 2 per cent lower than might otherwise have been sustained; it was

also estimated that our real gross national income would be
1.5 per cent down and our household consumption 2.5 per
cent less than might otherwise have been the case.[14] Quite
simply, outside we would all be poorer.

### Agriculture

Late entry into the EEC cost Britain the chance to influence
the design of the Common Agricultural Policy, which was
agreed by the Six during the 1960s. Despite the notoriety of
the CAP in Britain, there is nothing unusual about public
support for agriculture. EU subsidies amount to only 0.5 per
cent of GDP, or just 1 per cent of public spending, a smaller
portion than in neighbouring Norway or Switzerland and
less per farm than in Japan or the United States. Many British
farmers could not survive without the £3 billion a year they
get from the CAP, so removing support through the EU
would merely transfer the costs back to British taxpayers.

There is no doubt that the reputation of the CAP is one
of the principal reasons for the unpopularity of Europe in
Britain, and only by leading reform can we help put it right.
The ambition of British governments has consistently been
for a modern European framework that delivers a fair deal
for consumers, a decent income for farmers and proper protection for the environment. Progress, though slow, is being
made: successive waves of reform have cut the share of the
EU budget spent on the CAP from more than two-thirds in
the mid-1980s to less than half today, and the latest round
will slash prices to British consumers by £1 billion a year.[15]
The idea of unlimited support for unwanted production has
been gradually eliminated, putting an end to the infamous
butter mountains and wine lakes. Now there are new pressures for reform: recent health scares along with the prospect

of enlarging the EU to take in the largely agrarian economies of Central and Eastern Europe have prompted the most radical rethink yet. There is growing support for a move away from general subsidies based on the volume of production towards direct payments to farmers according to measures of quality and sustainable development. This would cut the bill and address the industrialisation of agriculture that has been partly blamed for the destruction of the countryside and problems like BSE and foot-and-mouth disease.

It is not only EU cash that British farmers bank on; they also depend on access to European consumers. Britain is one of the world's top ten food and drink exporters, and thanks to the internal market two-thirds goes to EU countries, as does three-quarters of our agricultural equipment exports. Britain's food and drink sales to the EU have trebled since we joined and are now worth £5 billion a year. That is why the National Farmers' Union has consistently supported our wholehearted membership.

Yet public perception is totally out of kilter with this reality. In recent years, much of that may be down to the fallout from the BSE crisis. As soon as it was known in March 1996 that scientific evidence linked the cattle disease to new variant CJD, a brain condition in humans, the European Commission imposed an immediate global ban on the sale of British beef. In the furore, the impression was created that the EU was somehow responsible for the spread of BSE in the first place. It was not; in fact, it provided 70 per cent of the compensation for removing older beef from the food chain, so helping to put an end to BSE in Britain. As the agency in charge of rules for both trade and public health, the Commission was properly responding to the problem.

The EU ban was lifted in August 1999. France, however,

has continued to foment anger by refusing to permit the sale of our beef. There are 102 other countries across the world (out of 189 members of the United Nations), which together comprise more than three-quarters of the population on earth (from Azerbaijan to the United States), that also still ban our beef. Unlike any of them, France is breaking the law. Against France, we have recourse to the European Court of Justice; although the wheels of justice are turning exasperatingly slowly, illustrating the need for reform, in the end France will be compelled to sell our beef by EU law. If we were not in the EU, we would have the same legal power over France that we have over the other 102: none whatsoever.

### Fisheries

Another price we paid for dithering over whether or not to join the EEC is that we had no say over the controversial Common Fisheries Policy, which was finalised on the very day that our accession negotiations began. This too has helped give Europe a bad name in Britain. While there are certainly problems with the CFP that need to be solved, the issues are not straightforward. Although the CFP has been blamed for the decline of British fishing, it is merely a policy response to the fact that too many boats are looking for too few fish in what have historically been mostly international waters.

The CFP granted trawlers registered in any EEC country the legal right to fish in grounds used by all member nations, except for limits extending twelve miles out from the coast. This meant that EEC trawlers could legally access parts of what had always been regarded, by convention but not by law, as British waters; it also meant that non-EEC countries, notably the Soviet Union, could no longer hoover the fish from our seas. However, when Iceland unilaterally estab-

lished a 200-mile limit in 1976, the 'cod war' broke out.
As we were prevented by the CFP from imposing our own
200-mile limit, our deep-sea fleet lost access to Icelandic
grounds but could not achieve a monopoly over ours in
compensation.

Anti-Europeans argue that Britain should simply withdraw from the EU and unilaterally declare our own 200-mile
limit. Apart from the fact that this is unfeasible because of our
geography – it would appropriate Irish grounds and cut deep
into the waters off the Norwegian fjords – it misunderstands
the problem that the CFP has been trying to address. Fish
stocks are scarce assets and a reduction or extinction of supplies would result in higher prices and fewer choices for
consumers as well as lost jobs in fishing communities and
damage to the underwater environment. So we would still
require limits to our catch. But restraint by British fishermen
alone would achieve nothing if others continued to net all
the fish. Fish do not respect national borders and a common
policy is the only way to protect these shared resources.
Although the CFP has faults and needs reform – especially to
improve enforcement – some kind of uncomfortable international agreement would be necessary whether we were in
the EU or not.

The fact is that Europe's fishermen, like others around the
world, are hauling far more fish than the waters can sustain.
As vessels have become more efficient, with advanced
locating and catching technology, capacity has to be cut. That
is why the CFP demands that between twelve and 200 miles
out from European coastlines countries are limited to quotas
as a proportion of the total allowable catch; incidentally,
Britain originally succeeded in obtaining a larger ration than
we were due according to our traditional catch levels,

especially over North Sea cod and haddock. The CFP also provides grants to compensate fishermen for decommissioning their boats, because fleets have to be reduced in size today if fish stocks and the fishing industry are to survive for tomorrow. Without action now, we would only pay an even higher price later on, as Canada is finding in waters where it has permitted over-fishing for too long.

## British quality of life

The Single Market liberated the movement of people as well as capital, goods and services. Britons now make about 35 million trips to the European Union each year, almost three times more than to the rest of the world. With the E111 scheme we are fully covered for emergency hospital treatment throughout Europe, just as we are under the NHS, and with passports for pets we can take our cats and dogs with us. Conversely, more than 15 million EU visitors annually come to Britain, spending £5 billion and helping sustain work for our 2 million tourist-industry employees.

While British football teams have been able to improve the strength of their squads because these days European players can come here more easily, almost half a million Britons now live in other EU countries. Of these, more than 100,000 are working, often having found employment through the EURES job search agency and with British qualifications that are recognised across Europe; another 200,000 are retired, taking advantage of the opportunity to draw their pensions anywhere in Europe; and a further 10,000 are studying or training with the help of programmes like ERASMUS.

Apart from these notable benefits for Britons abroad, the EU has also underpinned a better quality of life back home. We have much to learn from European achievements, from how to run a railway through to suppressing crime levels, generating a cleaner environment and tackling poverty. Thanks to the EU, which has promoted best practice, some of these standards are being raised in Britain too. We now have more rights at work and better rights as consumers, our local authorities have received billions of pounds for urban regeneration and social inclusion programmes, and much of our voluntary sector is increasingly dependent on accessing European decision-making and funding.

The case for European integration began simply as a means of ensuring peace by binding together the interests of countries that had so often been in destructive conflict with each other. In this task, it has been remarkably successful and it now has the historic chance to extend that ambition by securing stability and democracy in Central and Eastern Europe through enlargement. But the overwhelmingly powerful case for Britain in Europe today is not only that by working together we can help maintain peace, but that we can also maximise our prosperity and raise our living standards. In the twenty-first century the EU is emerging as the most appropriate vehicle to tackle a variety of other cross-borders problems and so improve our quality of life.

### Rights at work

European enterprises are compelled to restructure their operations to stay competitive in the internal market. They needed to become better at responding to economic change to match their rivals from America and Asia, but this has meant that weaker companies, older industries and poorer regions have felt the strain. Some workplaces have been hit hard and, especially as more national businesses become pan-European, workers require greater assistance to cooperate with progress and cope with the consequences of reform. It is no coincidence that in the European Union proposals for enhancing the social dimension emerged at the same time as moves for the single currency: the euro will make the pace of change even faster so a positive social agenda, promoting dialogue between firms and their employees, is vital.

The Social Chapter became a cause célèbre in Britain largely because John Major needed to be seen by his Euro-sceptic backbenchers to have come back with something from the controversial negotiations at Maastricht in 1991. Although he made great play of its alleged burdens on business and opted out, it is in fact a relatively innocuous instrument that barely raised a murmur from employers when Tony Blair opted into it in 1997.[16] The Social Chapter did not itself impose any new rules; instead, it extended Qualified Majority Voting to a limited number of areas like equal opportunities and working conditions, and more important it compelled the European Commission to consult with both sides of industry before initiating any proposals for consideration by the Council of Ministers. In other words, it instilled a new discipline in legislators because they now take decisions with advance knowledge of the opinions of management and labour.

European social legislation is not a rigid harmonising force – there is no prospect of interference on pay levels or trade union rights for example – but a flexible package of minimum standards compatible with different models of social and industrial organisation. The fact remains that it is generally cheaper and easier to make British workers redundant than their colleagues in other EU countries. Basic rights at work can stop structural change from turning industrial casualties into social outcasts and welfare dependants, helping those affected, even in the most extreme cases where modernisation means redundancies, still feel that they have a stake in society and can return to work.

The EU has promoted various mechanisms through which both sides of industry can work together, and with governments, in managing the process of change: at European works councils, at cross-sector meetings between the European employers' organisations UNICE and CEEP and the European TUC, and increasingly at sector level. The EU has begun to encourage respect for national and transnational trade union rights of association and collective bargaining, as laid out in the relevant International Labour Office Conventions. The folk memories of British industrial relations makes it easy to caricature this approach as at best time-wasting and at worst burdensome; but many of our most successful companies have shown that it works. Trade unions understand that employers need to be flexible to respond to fluctuations in demand, and they can do plenty to assist, such as negotiating annualised hours schemes and other modern working methods.

The vast bulk of legislation regulating the labour market is national. European laws simply set out minimum standards for matters such as health and safety, and British workers have directly gained from these in many ways. Women now have the right to equal pay thanks to a ruling in 1976 by the European Court of Justice; and 70,000 British women benefit every year from an EU agreement abolishing the requirement to work for two years for the same employer before qualifying for maternity leave.

Part-time and short-term workers have been granted full rights; and rules on the Transfer of Undertakings and Protection of Employment have guaranteed employee rights when companies are taken over, a process that must now involve consultation with workers. Most employees now have the right to a maximum average 48-hour working week, with minimum daily rest breaks and at least one day off each week, as well as unpaid parental leave. And more than three million Britons for the first time enjoy the right to four weeks' paid annual holiday.

This is a significant package of benefits to working people. In pretending that these basic rights, held by most workers throughout the industrialised world, have made British businesses uncompetitive, anti-Europeans are merely trying to substantiate the falsehood that the EU is an interfering 'superstate'. Yet there are enormous differences in the labour market between EU countries – for example the Netherlands has very light touch rules while Finland is heavily regulated, with Britain somewhere in between – which shows the room for manoeuvre at national level. In helping to raise the standards of the worst employers and the standard of living for millions of families across Britain the EU has played a constructive role. Leaving Europe would pull the rug from under their feet.

### Rights for consumers

Increased competition in the internal market has expanded the range of products and reduced the price of items in our shops. More than that, the European Union has boosted rights for consumers. We have long been afforded some protection by British Safety Standards, but now those minimum thresholds have been raised and extended across the whole of

Europe. For example, because of EU intervention we have higher standards of toy safety, better protection from credit card fraud, guaranteed compensation for overbooked airline seats and poor quality package tour holidays, and the ability to cancel any pressured purchase from doorstep or telephone salesmen.

European regulations also ensure that consumers have access to comprehensive information at the time of purchase. For instance, all foods must carry sell-by dates and a list of their ingredients, colourings and additives, and the green Eco-label identifies the most environmentally friendly products. In addition, a rapid warning system for cases of food contamination like BSE and foot-and-mouth disease is being established so that an outbreak in another country can be brought quickly to the attention of the British government in order for preventative action to be taken here.

Although there are examples of the EU seeking to interfere in unnecessary areas, it is often the perfectly sensible harmonisation of standards that provides material for myth-makers to distort these measures and undermine the credibility of Europe. In fact, harmonisation between EU countries benefits consumers and reduces the burdens on business because exporters are now required to meet a single benchmark rather than a number of different regulations.

### Crime and justice

Organised criminals, drug smugglers, football hooligans, people traffickers and terrorists are relatively modern scars on society. These are new threats that by their very nature transcend national borders. In extending its original objectives from promoting peace and trade, the European Union is well placed to tackle these and other international dangers to British law and order. Some members of the EU, through the Schengen Agreement of 1985, have taken steps to deal with asylum and immigration issues through common border controls, although because of our island status we have decided to maintain our own frontier controls.[17] Successive British governments have, however, been keen to establish cross-border cooperation on policing to clamp down on crime and enforce justice.

Europol, which was established in 1999, is not an independent operational force, let alone a European FBI, but a body to help facilitate better relations between national and local policing agencies. With its staff of just 300 – many seconded from EU members' forces – it is designed to gather, analyse and disseminate criminal intelligence. This involves no trespass of civil liberties and works in exactly the same way that Britain already shares privileged information with countries like Australia and the United States. That is why Europol has an office in Scotland Yard and British officers engage in its exchange programmes to train with the forces of other countries. This collaboration will be especially important when the EU enlarges to take in the former communist countries of Central and Eastern Europe, because their proximity to Russia will effectively make them Britain's furthest eastern border.

Europol officers will be able to take part in operations, but only in conjunction with local police forces. With a bigger budget and closer links to national agencies, it could become increasingly important. There has already been a series of successes, notably through teamwork at customs. Europol has particularly taken the lead against drug trafficking, seizing large quantities intended for Britain, and in stopping gangs from operating illegal immigration rackets. European cooperation also helped prevent serious trouble at Euro 2000 football matches, through the sharing of details on known troublemakers and spreading best practice in dealing with difficult crowd situations.

### Environmental protection

Pollution of the environment is another modern cross-border menace that can only be addressed by international agreement and common action. The European Union has introduced more than 200 conservation measures since Britain joined, its treaties have enshrined sustainable development and environmental protection as aims in law, and all major infrastructure developments initiated by the European Commission now have to be accompanied by exhaustive environmental impact assessments.

Although President George W. Bush pulled the United States out of the global deal reached at Kyoto in 1997, to the universal outrage of European leaders, EU heads of government have all agreed to stick to their target of cutting greenhouse gas emissions by 8 per cent by 2008–12. Europe has taken action to promote lead-free petrol and ensure that all new cars are fitted with catalytic converters; in consequence poisonous carbon monoxide emissions have receded by 40 per cent over the past decade and are set to shrink further. The EU has also led the way in cutting CFC chemicals that damage the ozone layer and sulphur diffusions that cause acid rain. Furthermore, local authorities now have to meet strict air quality targets to tackle the pollutants that affect asthma, bronchitis and nerve problems.

The EU is pressing for a ban on the testing of cosmetics on animals, which has already helped stimulate voluntary exclusion orders in Britain, while the setting of standards for transport conditions and the phasing out of battery hens have protected farm animals. The EU has promoted wildlife conservation and biological diversity in Europe and beyond, phasing out driftnets to protect dolphins, banning the import of whale products and seal-pup skins and improving the treatment of animals in zoos.

Britain has specifically benefited from EU environmental regulations. Ten years ago half of our bathing beaches failed to meet European standards, largely because of the discharge of raw sewage and toxic waste, but today 95 per cent are able to fly the 'blue flag' showing they are cleaner and safer. The EU has promoted bottle banks and recycling centres across the country, as well as providing emergency aid for fish farmers affected by the Shetlands oil spill in 1993 and special funding to support the ecological recovery of the Welsh coastline following the stranding of a Liberian tanker in 1996.

### Social cohesion

Unlike other European Union countries, Britain rarely recognises the enormous variety of buildings and open spaces that have been provided or improved with the assistance of EU grants. Only the biggest of these projects – like the Lowry Gallery in Manchester – ever gets much press coverage and very few have plaques or other symbols of acknowledgement, so hardly anyone knows whether their housing estate or local park have been helped by the EU. Yet there is barely a community in the country that has not gained in some way from the £14 billion that Britain has received for this purpose in the past decade.[18]

EU Structural Funds – chiefly the European Regional Development Fund and the European Social Fund – target assistance towards poor areas. They allocate money to top up that provided by national and local governments as well as businesses and charities. The structural funds totalled £22.5 billion in 1999, about one-third of the EU budget, and £2 billion came to Britain, the sixth largest beneficiary. We are set to receive another £10 billion over the next five years; of this, Wales will get £1.2 billion, Scotland £1 billion and Northern Ireland £600 million for peace and reconciliation programmes.

EU funds are helping to regenerate Britain's poorest regions. Northern Ireland, the Highlands and Islands, chunks of London and large swathes of Scotland, the North East, the North West and the West Midlands have long received help. Cornwall, Merseyside, South Yorkshire and two-thirds of Wales have recently qualified for what is known as 'Objective 1 status'; this means that they are among the poorest parts of Europe, with GDP per head 25 per cent below the average. In total the 5.5 million people living there will receive £3.3 billion of support.

EU funds also assist areas specifically blighted by industrial decline, given 'Objective 2 status'; they are largely channelled through local authorities and Regional Development Agencies. In the next five years, we will get £2.8 billion to tackle urban deprivation, rural poverty and the running down of fishing communities. A further £2.9 billion is available for education, training and employment programmes – 'Objective 3 status' – to address social exclusion.

Large areas of Britain are now deeply reliant on European structural funds for industrial recovery and social cohesion, and many voluntary organisations are increasingly dependent on EU grants for their work. Charities have been particularly successful in accessing the European Social Fund, in 1999 winning £80 million to finance 1,200 separate projects.

Without European help, many charities would go under and the people they help would suffer.

### The gateway to Europe, the bridge to the world

Anti-Europeans claim that by devoting energy to Europe, Britain is betraying its historic legacy as a Great Power and shrinking to nothing more than another second-division regional player. They argue that we are losing the status we enjoyed at the end of the Second World War and putting in jeopardy our ancestral connections to the United States and the Commonwealth. In saying this, they intend to foist on Britain a choice: to struggle on in Europe against an alleged Franco-German-dominated bloc that will always gang up on us, or to return to our rightful place as an independent force on the world stage. They hope that if confronted by this decision, Britons will reject the troublesome European Union in favour of the glory we enjoyed over fifty years ago.

This is a fantasy. We certainly punch above our weight in the international community: our permanent seat on the United Nations Security Council and our prominent position within NATO are testament to that. But we are not any more the Great Power that was the world's workshop, the ruler of a quarter of the planet's population or the winner of the world's wars. Relative economic decline, the end of Empire and the rise of the US as the dominant superpower saw to that. In truth, we are a great nation that has been through hard times and is on the way back again.

Ignoring Europe and discounting the resurrection of its battered economies during the 1950s and 1960s was part of the reason for our drift. Turning away again now would cause our recovery to falter. Europe is not a substitute for our other relationships, but neither can these other relationships replace the diplomatic authority we gain from the EU. Our place in the EU, the second-largest economic unit on earth, fortifies our other links. With our historic global reach Britain is the entry point to Europe for countries around the planet, not least because of our special relationship with the United States and our leadership of the Commonwealth, which provide a platform that few countries have. Far from being in conflict, these unique relations are bolstered by each other and to sacrifice any one of them would inevitably weaken the other two. We are taken more seriously in Europe because of our worldwide connections and we have greater influence around the globe because we are a leading player on the Continent: we are a bridge to the world precisely because we are a gateway to Europe. Yet because of our reluctance to appreciate the value of our European role, this is a position that we have barely started to exploit.

### Special relationship with the United States

Anti-Europeans particularly like to pretend that Britain must choose between our place in Europe and our special relationship with America. That is why they promote as an alternative membership of NAFTA and attack the idea of a European defence capability, even one that is set within NATO. They imply that international diplomacy is a zero-sum game: stronger links with the European Union must, they say, mean weaker ties with the United States. John Redwood has even gone so far as to write a whole book about what he claims are 'the coming conflicts between the USA and the European Union', based on his hypothesis that 'the

European project is born out of a strong anti-American-ism'.[19] But the premise is absurd and the dilemma is false, invented solely to help lever Britain out of Europe. Our standing in America is greater precisely because we have a powerful voice in Europe. We can have the best of both worlds as our continental and transatlantic relations are mutually reinforcing.

From the very start the US wanted Britain in the EEC, not least because we were seen as the most reliable friend, capable of unifying Europe as a bulwark against the threat of the Soviet Union. American leaders were perplexed at our hesitation over the Schuman Plan in 1950 and positively furious at our reluctance to help the Pleven Plan of 1951 develop into the proposed European Defence Community: President Dwight Eisenhower was even heard complaining that Britain was 'living in the past'.

It was partly in recognition of the squeeze on British influence caused by the shifting balance of power between America and Europe that Harold Macmillan made the first application to join. 'If we remain outside the European Community, it seems to me inevitable that the realities of power would compel our American friends to attach increasing weight to the views and interests of the Community, and to pay less attention to our own,' he wrote; 'we would find the United States and the Community concerting policy together on major issues, with much less incentive than now to secure our agreement or even consult our opinion. To lose influence both in Europe and Washington, as this must mean, would seriously undermine our international position.'[20]

When we finally did get in, the US was delighted. President Richard Nixon, like his predecessors, had offered discreet support and Secretary of State Henry Kissinger at last had a response to his famous question: 'When I want to speak to Europe, who do I call?' The answer these days is often the British prime minister. With our entangled history, shared interests and common language, Britain and America are natural partners, but access to the decision-making forums in Europe helped solidify the personal relations between Margaret Thatcher and Ronald Reagan then Tony Blair and Bill Clinton: US presidents know that they are talking not just to a sympathetic national politician but to an influential European and therefore world leader. 'America's transatlantic policy is European in scope. It is not a series of individual or compartmentalised bilateral policies, and never has been. It is the policy of one continent to another,' said Raymond Seitz, US ambassador to London, confirming Macmillan's theory of thirty years before. 'There is a simple observation that if Britain's voice is less influential in Paris or Bonn it is likely to be less influential in Washington.'[21]

With close friends in America and in Europe, Britain is in a unique pivotal position. We have often supported Washington's opinions in Brussels, recently over defence and security concerns in the Gulf and the former Yugoslavia. But we have also lobbied America for Europe's collective interests. For instance, at the height of the Cold War in 1982, when EU countries were working with the Soviet Union to build a pipeline to supply gas from Siberia to Western Europe, Thatcher managed to persuade Reagan to lift the US ban on trade in oil refining technology with the USSR.

Our role in Europe makes us more attractive to the US economically as well as diplomatically. The EU and the US are each other's major business partners: in 2000 Europe exported goods and services worth £214 billion to America while the US exported £184 billion to the EU. One in

twelve American factory workers are employed in the 4,000
European-owned businesses in the US – Europeans are the
biggest foreign investors in 41 of the 50 states – and Ameri-
can-owned companies employ 3 million people in Europe.
Over 40 per cent of US inward investment into the EU
comes to Britain, largely as a base from which factories
export to the rest of Europe, and the 2,500 American companies located here now employ almost one million of our
workers.

This all makes the currently fashionable notion of leaving
the European Union for the North American Free Trade
Agreement rather silly. Phil Gramm, an eccentric Texas
senator and friend of John Redwood, recently requested that
the US International Trade Commission investigate the
likely impact of Britain joining NAFTA, in the hope that it
would recommend such a move. In fact, it rejected the idea
out of hand, reporting that 'were the UK to have a different
relationship with the EU, the UK might not only face
uncertainty in its trade and investment with the rest of the
EU, but might also face uncertainty in its trade relationships
with the rest of the world'.[22]

Britain and America have undoubted historic and cultural
connections that have allowed us to forge a genuinely inti-
mate special relationship. But in the realpolitik of the
modern world, Britain is most important to the US as a leading European player. We should use that crucial position to
advance our own national interests, promoting the values we
share with America in Europe and encouraging the EU to
sign deals with NAFTA that promote free trade between the
two continents.[23] To choose between the two is not only
unnecessary, it would also be damaging to our influence and
our economy.

*Defence and security*

Another world war on the ancient battlefields of Central Europe is now unthinkable. The military might of the North Atlantic Treaty Organisation, in deterring aggression by the Soviet Union, and the economic bond of the European Union, in reconciling the interests of France and Germany, have together maintained unprecedented peace on the Continent for more than half a century, just as the founding fathers envisaged. In that time, American leadership of NATO has been greatly assisted by the steadfastness of Britain, and Germany, in resisting repeated French initiatives to pull free of US control.

Yet the end of the Cold War has reoriented American foreign policy priorities. The US is not completely withdrawing from Europe, although the number of its troops on the Continent has been cut from 320,000 to 100,000 in the past decade; but as Russia is increasingly considered an unstable irritant more than a potential invader, Europe has inevitably declined as a vital area of American strategic interest. Bill Clinton and even more so George W. Bush have made clear that their primary military concerns now lie in Asia, particularly the latent strength of China and the potential nuclear threat of North Korea. Currently the biggest security issue in the US is how to develop a missile defence system that shields against nuclear attack from rogue states, regardless of European worries that it may reignite the global arms race. As the power base of American politics shifts away from New England to the South West, and as Pacific and Latin influences increase, the logical corollary is that Europe is being urged to take greater responsibility for our own security in our own back yard.

Margaret Thatcher saw this coming as long ago as 1984.

'Our objective must be to strengthen the European pillar of the Alliance and improve European defence cooperation,' she wrote in a paper for the European Council.[24] By the time Michael Portillo became Defence Secretary in 1996, this ambition was coming to fruition; on top of a tentative Common Foreign and Security Policy a specific defence initiative emerged. 'An essential part of this adaptation is to build a European Security and Defence Identity within NATO, which will enable all European Allies to make a more coherent and effective contribution to the missions and activities of the Alliance as an expression of our shared responsibilities,' read the NATO communiqué that he signed, 'to act themselves as required; and to reinforce the transatlantic partnership.'[25] Despite, or perhaps because of, a surfeit of security bodies – among them the Organisation for Security and Cooperation in Europe and the Western European Union – Europe has been too reliant on the US for too long. And Britain is a European country by dint of geography, whatever our other political loyalties may be.

Notwithstanding these good intentions, the EU has continued to depend heavily on the US, notably in the Bosnian tragedy. And lack of firepower constrained the EU in Kosovo, despite the reluctance of the US to commit ground forces or to undertake intensive peacekeeping functions; it was then that Britain acted as the bridge between Brussels and Washington as Tony Blair was able to urge American action in defence of an essentially European interest.

This poor show encouraged Blair to try to strengthen the capacity of EU countries to respond promptly and effectively to local threats, making real Thatcher's and Portillo's earlier promises. European troops already comprise 80 per cent of the peacekeeping forces in the Balkans and in 1998 Britain and France signed the St Malo Accord to agree the formal outline of a European defence force: to be set within NATO but operable under the direction of EU governments when the US and thus NATO does not want to become militarily involved, and to draw on NATO assets with the agreement of its non-EU members. This plan, developed in close consultation with the US and NATO, was then endorsed by the EU as a whole in 2000. The Rapid Reaction Force will not have an offensive role; it is designed to put 60,000 troops into any trouble spot within sixty days to carry out humanitarian or peacekeeping tasks. It has nothing whatsoever to do with collective defence, the raison d'être of NATO for fifty years.

Although anti-Europeans have claimed that the Rapid Reaction Force is a threat to NATO and endangers our special relationship with the US, this is certainly not a concern shared across the Atlantic. 'Creation of this capability promises to improve Europe's ability to act in ways that will strengthen European and transatlantic security. It is a key feature of the European Security and Defence Identity, a NATO initiative that the US has supported wholeheartedly. This EU force will be available to both NATO and the EU, in those cases where the Alliance as a whole is not militarily engaged. It offers a valuable complement to the efforts and capabilities of NATO,' said Madeleine Albright, Secretary of State under Bill Clinton.[26] 'The United States supports and welcomes the creation of a European defence facility, and believes that as long as it avoids duplication measures and has some kind of joint planning arrangements with NATO that it will enhance and strengthen the alliance's capabilities,' said Colin Powell, Secretary of State under George W. Bush, ensuring the line remained the same even when the administration changed.[27]

The Rapid Reaction Force has also been strongly supported by NATO as a whole: its official response announced
that 'we welcome the further impetus that has been given to
the strengthening of European defence capabilities to enable
the European Allies to act more effectively together, thus
reinforcing the transatlantic partnership'.[28] George Robert-
son, Secretary-General of NATO, added that 'the EU plans
are, in my view, no danger to NATO's future; indeed, they
will guarantee NATO's continued relevance and success'.[29]

There is complete consensus between the EU, the US and
NATO over the need for a stronger defence capability to deal
with situations in Europe that are of no direct concern to
America. While it is true that there has been debate about
detail between Britain and France – notably over the nature of
its planning function – even Jacques Chirac, the French President, commented that 'any suggestion of an opposition
between the Atlantic Alliance and the construction of
Europe would be a historical nonsense'.[30] At the top table in
Europe, Britain can continue to support US and NATO
interests while at the same time shaping moves towards a
greater capacity to protect ourselves. Outside, we would be
mere bystanders as this crucial initiative developed without us.

Anti-Europeans have been trying to use the Rapid Reaction Force to drive a wedge between Europe and America as
a way of forcing Britain to choose between the two. Worse
than historical nonsense, this is dangerously irresponsible. A
strong partnership between Europe and America, which
Britain helps to buttress, remains essential for global stability
and progress.

### Unique links to the Commonwealth
Britain's Imperial legacy has bequeathed a global reach that

extends far beyond that of similar-sized countries. In addition to our special relationship with the US and our key role in NATO, we enjoy unique links to those 53 countries around the world that comprise the Commonwealth.

The possible impact of European integration on the Commonwealth was a major factor in Britain's initial reluctance to join the Schuman Plan or the Messina Conference. It especially worried patrician Tories in the 1950s such as Anthony Eden and Labour anti-Marketeers during the 1960s like Hugh Gaitskell and Harold Wilson. Given that the Commonwealth was then brand new – it was formed in 1949 – and many colonies were still claiming independence, an unsettling process for many British leaders as they watched the Suez crisis blow up in their face and the Empire shrink on the map, this is unsurprising.

Harold Macmillan devoted considerable effort to assuaging the concerns of Commonwealth leaders. He received delegation after delegation and he even titled his crucial pamphlet outlining the reasons for his application *Britain, the Commonwealth and Europe*. In it, he rightly argued that 'our main economic value to the Commonwealth countries is our ability to provide a large market for their goods and to supply them with funds for their development. A Britain which gains in strength from membership of the Common Market, as I believe we would, would be in a much better position to help the Commonwealth than a Britain living in political and economic isolation from Europe'.[31]

Many Commonwealth countries were nervous at the beginning, anxious that their preferential access to British markets for their foodstuffs and raw materials should not be impaired. In fact, the years of delay meant France was able to argue that British dependencies, unlike French ones, should not be permitted automatic special treatment. During the talks that led to entry in 1973, Commonwealth questions featured heavily and in the end there were two major sticking points: Caribbean sugar and New Zealand butter. These economies largely depended on the sale of these commodities in Britain, so we paid a price to ensure that they were not damaged by entering the customs union.

Despite the problems, Arnold Smith, Secretary-General of the Commonwealth, caught the prevailing mood when he declared 'I believe that British EEC entry will make the Commonwealth more important, not less so, to [its] members.'[32] He has been proved right. British membership opened fresh avenues of influence to them, most of their preferences were eventually maintained and they have benefited enormously from European funds.

Not only does the EU generate the most trade in the world, it also grants the most aid. Together with the member states, it accounts for more than half of all official international development assistance, two-thirds of all grant aid and more humanitarian relief than anyone else, much of which has gone to Commonwealth countries. In 2000 Europeans contributed the equivalent of £45 each, compared to the £15 donated by each American.

These days, for Britain the prop of the Commonwealth has weakened and it is certainly no substitute for the standing we get from playing a leading role in Europe. Conversely, it confers an additional authority that Europe cannot provide. It is still a force for stability, promoting liberal democracy around the world, and Britain remains the beneficiary of much Commonwealth trade and investment, frequently as the filter to European markets. For example, of the exports Australia and Canada send to the EU one-third are sold in

Britain, and of their investments into the EU 60 per cent of Australia's and 45 per cent of Canada's come to Britain. Without access to the internal market we would be a far less appealing destination, because tariffs and regulations would be imposed on their exports from Britain to the rest of the Continent.

Britain is certainly stronger because of our place at the head of the Commonwealth and at the side of the United States. But of the three circles of influence that guided foreign policy after the Second World War, Europe has become by far the most important to us. The EU has not, nor ever will, replace the others, but as we are at the intersection of all three it enables us to stand taller than we otherwise would. As an interlocutor between them all, we are an invaluable channel of influence. To throw all this away because of anti-European prejudices would undercut our standing in the world and undermine our national interests.

The benefits Britain derives from its membership of the European Union are often mundane and rarely the stuff of rabble-rousing rhetoric. Added together, however, they significantly improve our prosperity, our quality of life and our international influence. And this package is exceptional value for money. In 2000 EU membership cost each of us an average of 15 pence per day, half as much as a television licence, compared to the £16.50 a day that the average citizen gave to the British government; we also got £2 billion back in a budget rebate, which means that since the mechanism was agreed in 1984 we have received £30 billion.

Yet practically every advantage has been derided by anti-Europeans. They have allowed their ideological hostility to get in the way of an honest cost-benefit analysis, preventing them from judging any issue on its own terms. They censure every measure, from cleaner beaches to safer food, as 'proof' that the EU is a 'superstate' trying to undermine our traditional way of life. Contrary to their professed support for free trade, they would even destroy the internal market by sweeping away the European Court of Justice that is needed to enforce it. Because their declamations are more newsworthy than the individual measures they revile, the catalogue of EU benefits has got lost in a media frenzy.

The European Union is far from perfect. But membership has been overwhelmingly favourable for us, as individuals and as a nation. If we started to realise the profit we have already taken from it, we could begin to get even more out of it. After years of prevarication, we finally overcame our fears and, whether we liked it or not, accepted that our future is inexorably and inevitably tied up with developments on the Continent. Anti-Europeans would have us unlearn the lessons of history and throw away all the hard-won gains, for the sake of their dogma. They have been using the single currency, which could generate even greater benefits for Britain, to whip up fears of Europe and disrupt confidence in our place in the EU. It is high time that reason overcame hysteria in the debate about Britain and Europe.

# The Single Currency

## The evolution of the euro

The agony of indecision over the single currency has afflicted Britain since the fall of Margaret Thatcher. It paralysed John Major's government, splitting the Tory Party and helping render it unelectable, and it has undermined Tony Blair's claim to strong leadership in Britain and in Europe. We have managed to postpone the decisive moment for a decade, after negotiating an opt-out from the Maastricht Treaty, but we must soon actively choose whether or not to join, else we will be left behind by default.

In October 1997 Gordon Brown, the Chancellor, told Parliament that the Government 'believe that, in principle, British membership of a successful single currency would be beneficial'.[1] To determine the precise timing of entry, he identified five economic tests that need to be met before the Government will recommend a Yes vote in a referendum. Although these tests have been criticised as subjective – and

104 MADE IN BRITAIN

there can never be a mathematically definitive calculation either way – they will in fact lead to a balanced conclusion. And they rightly examine the issues that any sensible person would think important: are the British and European economies in synch, could we deal with any problems if they arise, and would it be better for investment, for the City of London and for jobs.[2] After all, if the economic conditions are not right, only a fool would want to risk our economy; if they are favourable, however, only dogmatists would turn their backs on the chance to improve our prosperity.

### Currency volatility

Since the early nineteenth century, when foreign trade took off, Britain has spent most of the time without a fully floating exchange rate. As in other industrialised economies, the government has usually tried to manage the currency by fixing its value through international agreements. This is simply because while a fully floating exchange rate allows the interest rate to be changed to dampen or stimulate demand, frequent and unpredictable shifts in the value of the currency are a prime cause of economic instability. This point lies behind the case in principle for a single currency across a broader trading area than Britain's domestic market.

With floating exchange rates, the profitability of all businesses that export abroad or compete against imports at home partly depends on the value of the currency: too high a rate leads to a loss of competitiveness and eventually to redundancies and bankruptcies, too low a rate makes imports expensive and nourishes inflation, and repeated jerks from high to low and back again hamper business planning and inject instability into the economy. Some protection can be afforded against the risk of currency fluctuations by hedging in the forward exchange markets, commonly through futures contracts, but they are very costly and usually limited to short time periods. As it is not possible to insure fully, the possibility of currency gyrations deters long-term investment and hinders medium-sized enterprises from expanding abroad.

Britain has historically judged these fundamentals to be sufficiently important to warrant entering a variety of managed or pegged systems. This was the purpose of the Gold Standard after 1821, the Bretton Woods Agreement of 1944, the Snake in the 1970s and the Intergovernmental Agreements of the 1980s. The most recent example was the notorious Exchange Rate Mechanism, which came into operation in 1979.

### The Exchange Rate Mechanism

Under the ERM, the currencies of member countries were supposedly 'fixed' within predetermined fluctuation bands of plus or minus 2.25 per cent against a central denominator, the European Currency Unit. The ECU was a basket of these currencies, weighted to roughly reflect the relative size of the member countries' economies. All members were required to set their interest rates and use their foreign currency reserves to maintain their agreed exchange rates. These currency values were also 'adjustable' because realignments were allowed with the unanimous consent of the participants. After a bout of initial realignments, the ERM underpinned a period of remarkable currency stability and strong growth during the mid- to late 1980s. However, it was to end in disaster for Britain on Black Wednesday.[3]

Since 16 September 1992 some have argued that Britain's ejection from the ERM shows why we should not join the euro. They rightly contend that the government was

compelled to raise interest rates to sustain the value of the
pound just when it should have been cutting them to avert
recession; then they add that our departure and devaluation
liberated the economic recovery that had been held back. But
their underlying premise, that the single currency is nothing
but a facsimile of the ERM, and their conclusion that we
should not repeat the same mistake, are simply wrong.

In fact, the recession was brought about by domestic
policy failures, a model of boom and bust. Nigel Lawson, the
Chancellor, fuelled consumer spending in 1988 by deregulat-
ing personal credit, slashing income taxes and chopping
interest rates, thus pumping an inflationary bubble that later
propelled interest rates back up again. Britain then joined
the ERM for the wrong reasons: largely because Margaret
Thatcher was losing Britain's influence in Europe, relegated
to a permanent minority of one at the critical moment when
plans were formed to deal with the consequences of German
reunification. At the wrong time: thanks to the Lawson
boom-bust our economic cycle slipped out of kilter with
that of our main trading partners just before we entered in
1990 because by then Britain was expanding rapidly as Germany constrained policy to cope with reunification. At the
wrong rate: rather than negotiating a competitive value
Thatcher insisted on a virility symbol and DM2.95 was far
too high because it could not be sustained by our economic
performance.

Once inside, the Public Sector Borrowing Requirement
soared to £35 billion and inflation peaked at 10.9 per cent. A
classic sterling crisis ensued, with the pound overvalued and
bound to crash. Nor did merely leaving the ERM bring
about lasting recovery. Without fiscal and monetary tighten-
ing, the devaluation – sterling lost 15 per cent of its value in

six months, shrinking to DM2.35 – was bound to cause another bogus boom. Instead, borrowing and inflation steadily receded thanks to a series of tax and interest rate hikes that cost the Conservatives any chance of winning the 1997 election.

The central lesson of the ERM fiasco is that traditional exchange rate management through pegged systems is no longer viable in the era of globalisation. Norman Lamont, the Chancellor, wrongly believed in 1992 that he could maintain the value of the currency merely by raising interest rates and buying pounds with foreign exchange reserves. In just one day he put up base rates from 10 to 15 per cent and spent about £15 billion.[4] But economic fundamentals matter, and the powers of modern financial markets are so great that as Thatcher said they simply cannot be bucked.

By 1992 the assets of international institutions had rocketed in thirty years from 10 per cent of the value of world trade to more than 200 per cent. This colossal strength, unleashed by the abolition of exchange controls in 1979 and the Big Bang in the City of London in 1986, overpowered the Government's muscle. The Bank of England's foreign currency reserves were at a comparatively high level in 1992 but they still came to only 5 per cent of the value of the assets of British institutions, never mind those from around the world.

The vast majority of assets sloshing around the foreign exchanges come from the savings of ordinary families, in pension funds and insurance companies. Prudent management of these investments requires constant assessments of potential exchange rate movements, and even small percentage shifts from one currency to another can themselves trigger an avalanche in the relative value of currencies. Once the markets decided the exchange rate was wrong in 1992, the maths did not add up. The Government did not have sufficient resources to resist panic among asset managers. Speculators, who had a simple target to attack that could not be defended – the sterling value of DM2.95 – were then faced by a one-way bet. Although sterling's rate was fixed in theory, it turned out to be all too adjustable in practice.

Since then the capital markets have swelled even further. More than £40 billion sweeps through the foreign exchanges each hour of every day, seldom reflecting relative changes in the underlying performance of economies; instead these movements are frequently motivated by groundless expectations about what may or may not happen in two or three years' time. Confronted by such relatively irrational capacity, governments are impotent and pegged systems are untenable. So the choice for modern trading economies is between a fully floating exchange rate and fixed-but-not-adjustable systems like Economic and Monetary Union. Ironically, the failure of the ERM therefore makes the single currency even more attractive.

### The Maastricht Treaty

The Maastricht Treaty identified a means of abolishing exchange rate changes and therefore currency movements between members of the European Union: by establishing a single currency and a single monetary policy under a European Central Bank. This has the added advantage of expunging the costs of changing money from one currency to another, which the European Commission estimates amount to an average of 0.4 per cent of GDP, a potential saving to Britain of £3.6 billion a year.[5] By circumventing the costs of currency transactions and the risks of exchange rate changes, which are just as much a barrier to trade as tariffs and regulations, Economic and Monetary Union completes the internal market: within the euro-zone is an area of guaranteed currency stability, insulated from speculative attack in a way that pegged systems like the ERM could not deliver.

Although Britain and Denmark opted out of this section of the Treaty, ten countries – Belgium, France, Germany, Greece, Ireland, Italy, Luxembourg, the Netherlands, Portugal and Spain – committed themselves to achieving Economic and Monetary Union by 1999. When three new members acceded to the EU in 1995, Austria and Finland also opted into EMU while Sweden did not.

The Treaty outlined five convergence criteria to ensure that all participating economies would be more or less in synch. As a condition of entry budget deficits were to be less than 3 per cent of GDP and levels of public debt below or falling towards 60 per cent of GDP. In addition, the criteria specified there must be convergent inflation, convergent interest rates and stable exchange rates. Despite widespread scepticism that the criteria were too tough to meet and that there would be cheating, eleven nations sufficiently impressed the markets with their achievements to allow interest rates to fall back to post-war lows. The applicants proved their ability to take reform seriously when hard economic and political realities demanded. Italy, for example, reduced its budget deficit from more than 10 per cent of GDP in 1991 to 2 per cent by 1997. Only Greece initially failed to fulfil the criteria, but after further reform it joined the other eleven in the euro in 2001.

Ignoring the lessons of the Schuman Plan and the Messina Conference, on 1 January 1999 Britain watched from the sidelines as eleven economies locked their exchange rates.

The single currency was smoothly launched and the euro became a reality in the financial markets; national currencies are to be phased out and replaced by euro cash in January and February 2002. Against the turbulent sweep of European history, it was an extraordinary achievement. Almost 300 million people, divided by eight official languages and spread across eleven sovereign nations that had spent much of the century at war with each other, pooled their national currencies in Economic and Monetary Union.

## The birth of the euro

Over the first twenty-two months of its life the euro lost 30 per cent of its value against the dollar, tumbling from $1.17 to 83 cents by October 2000. In Britain this was widely portrayed as a sign of weakness, even of failure; anti-Europeans rejoiced as it became extremely difficult for the benefits of the single currency in principle to receive a decent hearing in public debate. Yet this collapse was of surprisingly little consequence to the euro-zone economies themselves.

At the time of the launch, on most measures of relative costs and prices the euro was significantly overvalued against the dollar and market correction was inevitable. The United States was enjoying a period of growth that seemed so robust commentators routinely described it as an 'economic miracle'. Meanwhile, Europe was still scrambling out of a recession prolonged by German reunification and the wholesale restructuring needed to meet the Maastricht criteria. The fledgling currency started to fall to properly reflect the balance of strength in the real economies of the US and the euro-zone, assisted by investment opportunities and more attractive interest rates in America. It was then pulled even lower because the markets found it difficult to interpret the uncertain signals sent by the newly formed European Central Bank.

Following the tendency of exchange rates to overshoot reasonable adjustments, the euro became significantly undervalued. Bullish dealers, who at the beginning of 1999 declared that it would quickly supplant the dollar as the most popular reserve currency in the world, turned bearish and within a year started referring to it as a 'toilet paper currency'. Such wild emotions do not square with the economic fundamentals, however, and a further market correction to restore fair value is likely over the medium term, not least because of the slowdown in the American economy from the start of 2001.

After the US, the euro-zone is the largest economic unit in the world. By adopting the single currency the twelve members have effectively internalised the vast majority of their trade, dramatically cutting their exposure to the vagaries of currency movements. Exports outside the euro-zone are now equivalent to just over 10 per cent of its GDP, a similar proportion to the US, whereas previously those of France and Germany to all other countries were equal to nearly 30 per cent each, similar to Britain's. Like the US Federal Reserve, therefore, the ECB can now happily follow a policy of almost 'benign neglect' to the exchange rate without unduly troubling the economy.

In its first two years, the euro-zone performed strongly, certainly compared to Britain. Average growth rates were 2.5 per cent in 1999 and 3.5 per cent in 2000, against 2.2 per cent and 3.1 per cent in Britain. Along with structural reforms to the supply side, this has helped reduce unemployment. A net 3 million new jobs were created in the euro-zone, where the number of jobs is annually expanding by 1.8 per cent against

0.9 per cent in Britain. Although unemployment levels are still too high, a corner seems to have been turned. As the value of the euro affects such a small proportion of the traded economy, its fall has had little impact on prices. Inflation averaged 2.3 per cent in 2000, low even by the historic standards of Germany, where inflation has averaged 3.4 per cent since 1960. This has allowed euro-zone interest rates to be held down below those in Britain and the US.

Far from worrying about the value of the euro, its members have benefited from a competitive currency, enjoying their best economic record for ten years. Although as the US catches cold, Europe has inevitably sniffled if not actually sneezed, the Continent is becoming better insulated from the repercussions of falling demand from across the Atlantic.

## Arguments for joining

The debate about the single currency in Britain often seems stuck in a time warp. It is no longer sufficient to consider whether or not Economic and Monetary Union is desirable. That argument raged in the years from the Delors Report to Maastricht to the birth of the euro. It is now necessary to examine the consequences of Britain signing up to or staying out of a system that is already used by twelve of our biggest trading partners in our primary trading association, the European Union.[6]

### Sterling's volatility
When the Common Market was launched one pound was worth fourteen francs or twelve deutschmarks. By the time France and Germany entered the single currency one

pound bought just nine francs or three deutschmarks. Over the same period, sterling lost about half its value against the dollar and five-sixths its value against the yen. Beneath this headline of depreciation, sterling has lurched from one crisis to another on an unpredictable rollercoaster. Apart from the formal devaluations of 1949 and 1967, when it was adjusted by 31 per cent and 14 per cent respectively, a run on the pound in 1976 forced it down by almost 30 per cent over six months, provoking the crunch that ended with Britain in debt to the International Monetary Fund. More recently, with a fully floating exchange rate, sterling has suffered periods of equally damaging overvaluation and undervaluation.

Between 1979 and 1981 it climbed by 14 per cent against the dollar and by 30 per cent against the deutschmark. This abetted a recession in manufacturing that dragged output down by 15 per cent and investment down by 30 per cent as blue-chip companies like ICI recorded losses for the first time in their history and unemployment virtually trebled to 3 million. The Treasury's response to the high pound in 1981 was to put up taxes and hack back interest rates, cutting the value of sterling by 17 per cent in six months. It cascaded from a high of $2.40 to a low of $1.01, until in 1985 Margaret Thatcher panicked at the humiliating prospect of reaching parity with the dollar. To address the problem, the Treasury lifted interest rates again. After further rocky patches – for instance, in 1989 sterling was worth DM3.28 in January but just DM2.72 in December, another descent of 17 per cent – the next upheaval resulted from leaving the Exchange Rate Mechanism. The pound went into free fall, swooping from DM2.95 in 1992 to DM2.22 in 1995, a significant undervaluation.

Since the advent of the single currency sterling has been even more unpredictable. George Soros, the arbitrage specialist who reputedly made $1 billion on Black Wednesday, forecast in 1998 that if a single currency was set up without Britain then the pound would be squeezed between two constantly shifting tectonic plates, the euro and the dollar. 'I think that sterling will be in that case in a very dangerous position,' he said, 'more volatile and more unstable, in my view, because it would be caught between these two large currency zones.' He added that 'if the value of sterling diverged very much from the euro, which constitutes the main trading partner of sterling, it would create dislocations. I also think that sterling could become more subject to speculative attacks, if you like, attacks or speculative movements, which would drive it in one direction or another too far'.[7] That is exactly what has happened. At times it has been simultaneously at a fifteen-year high against the euro and its predecessors (escalating to €1.74 or DM3.40) and a fifteen-year low against the dollar (falling as far as $1.40).

Apart from the scale of currency fluctuations, several factors determine the extent of their impact on an economy. One is its size: the bigger the economy the better insulated it is because the greater its ability to cushion any blows. On this score, Britain is significantly more vulnerable than the euro-zone or the United States. Although Britain has the fourth or fifth largest economy in the world, with a GDP of £900 billion, this is a lot smaller than that of the euro-zone, £4,000 billion, and of the US, £5,500 billion, so we have much less ability to absorb exchange rate shocks.

The other elements relate to the proportion and distribution of trade. While the euro-zone and the US each export the equivalent of only about one-tenth of GDP, Britain is a historic trading nation that exports nearly one-third. Furthermore, we are becoming more reliant on foreign trade: since we joined the Common Market our trade has expanded much faster than our growth. The euro-zone and the US also have greater dispersion of trade across the globe, making their exchange rate with any one trading partner relatively insignificant. Conversely, British trade is increasingly concentrating on one partner, the European Union. Since 1973 the proportion of our goods exported to the EU has jumped from 35 per cent to 57 per cent, while only 16 per cent goes to the US and just 12 per cent goes to Asia. In fact, more than half our total trade in goods is with the euro-zone.[8]

This mattered less when the EU countries each had their own currencies because the risk was spread. For example, dislocations between the pound and the lira did not necessarily affect trade between Britain and Spain. Now that all but Denmark and Sweden share the same currency, British trade is heavily focused on a single currency area. This is likely to become even more intense as many of the applicants for EU membership may well soon adopt the euro too. Furthermore, as the euro creeps into common usage here – whether we officially join or not – the profitability of British businesses will become still more tied to its value vis-à-vis sterling. Day-trippers to Dover and tourists in London will want to shop with euros and retailers are already preparing to accept euro cash, while multinationals operating across Europe such as Philips and Unilever are beginning to invoice and account in euros to cut costs.

The very fact that so many of our leading trading partners have adopted the single currency, whether we wanted them to or not, has made sterling more volatile and joining the euro more attractive as the solution to the problem. This explains why the Euro-sceptics in the early 1990s sought not just to prevent Britain signing up to the single currency but also to derail the whole project and stop the euro coming about by rejecting the Maastricht Treaty.

The extent of our trade explains why we have historically suffered disproportionately from currency gyrations. The pattern of our trade shows why the relationship between sterling and the euro has become far more important than that between sterling and the dollar or the yen, making it unusually central to our national stability and prosperity. Britain is therefore far more vulnerable than before, and much more exposed than our chief competitors, to the consequences of currency volatility. By staying out Britain is being left at a unique competitive disadvantage.

### Exports

During the first two years of the euro our economy performed strongly, though weaker than the euro-zone. Yet the giddiness of sterling remains a serious source of instability because even outside the single currency we cannot avoid its impact. When the euro plunged against the dollar, sterling was caught in the crossfire, just as George Soros predicted. The euro lost 18 per cent of its value against the pound, diving from 70 pence to 56.8 pence by May 2000. Another way of looking at it is that the pound soared by more than 20 per cent, reaching the equivalent of DM3.40, 15 per cent above the heady height at which Britain left the ERM.

It does not matter if this disequilibrium is blamed on the 'low euro' or the 'high pound' because the consequences are identical. The situation is similar to when the United States devalued under the Bretton Woods system in 1971: Britain complained that sterling was left painfully high, but John Connally, US Treasury Secretary, replied, 'It may be our dollar, but it's your problem.' And the problem of the disequilibrium between the euro and the pound has been felt much more keenly in Britain than in the euro-zone, inflicting searing pain on swathes of British industry and leaving our economy significantly unbalanced, with private demand booming but output sluggish.

The British Tourist Authority estimates that the appreciation of sterling means that its industry has missed out on £2 billion in revenue and 70,000 jobs. The high pound has also added to the distress of the farming community. Two-thirds of our food and drink exports go to the EU but during 1999 and 2000 sales slumped, helping destroy the equivalent of 34,000 full-time jobs.[9] Furthermore, British farmers receive £3 billion a year in CAP subsidies, but because they are paid in euros the happenchance of the high pound means that they have got far less than they would have done with a low one.[10]

In steelworking, Corus lost over £1 billion in 2000 and consequently cut a total of 10,500 jobs across the country, a third of its workforce, largely blaming the high pound for the collapse of orders and the closure of sites. In textiles, almost 30,000 jobs in 1999 and nearly 40,000 jobs in 2000 were lost. A report by the Textile and Clothing Strategy Group, commissioned by the Department of Trade and Industry, concluded that 'recent adverse exchange rates have had a profound impact upon the export performance of the sector and the ability of domestic companies to compete against imports'.[11] In motor manufacturing, although various historic problems contributed to the troubles of Rover at Longbridge, the high pound was responsible for a third of its £6 million daily losses. Rover was sold by BMW to Phoenix on 17 March 2000 for £10, with the loss of 4,500 jobs; in a simple illustration of the impact of currency fluctuations, by the time Phoenix sent the cheque a week later sterling had slumped and with the added transaction costs they actually paid £10.36.

Less well known than these and other high-profile casualties that have damaged our fragile manufacturing base are the tragedies that have befallen thousands of little firms, many of which do not deal with Europe at all. More than 750,000 small and medium-sized enterprises are connected to Europe, either trading directly or indirectly as suppliers to larger exporters. When big businesses lose sales and cut back, everyone in the supply chain, from components manufacturers to cleaning contractors, also suffers. For example, within weeks of the sale of Rover, tyre production at Fort Dunlop in Birmingham stopped, with the loss of 600 jobs. And as the high pound made euro-zone goods cheaper, many British-based companies switched to buying their supplies from the Continent, taking orders away from local SMEs.

### Inward investment

Before the euro all EU currencies carried an exchange rate risk against each other, so when non-EU firms decided where in Europe to base their production Britain presented no greater hazard than any other member. But now that twelve countries are establishing an area of guaranteed currency stability covering 300 million consumers, the scales are tipping against us, creating a unique gamble for inward investors looking for a gateway to Europe.

This is why, despite our language, enterprise environment and many other attractions, so many American, Japanese and other companies have been warning of the dangers if Britain stays out in the long term. The threat was highlighted in May 2000 in a leaked memo from Andrew Fraser, chief executive of the Invest in Britain Bureau, the agency designed to attract inward investors. He noted that up to 75 per cent of investors' production in Britain is exported, primarily to the euro-zone, and he reported that they repeatedly tell him 'we have to have our cost base denominated in the same currency as our principal revenues', which is why he wrote 'I have yet to meet a single inward investor in manufacturing who would like us to stay outside.' He predicted that if we do stay out then 'we must now expect a significant level of high-profile closures', a 'loss of major inward investors' and a '"meltdown" of major manufacturing sectors'.[12]

This miserable prognosis was endorsed in June 2000 in another leaked memo, this time from Stephen Gomersall, ambassador to Tokyo, about his efforts to attract Japanese firms to Britain. He flagged that 'companies are beginning to see pound/euro unpredictability as a long-term disincentive to investment in Britain,' feeding 'a generalised perception that, until the UK is clearly on a track to join the single currency, further investment in the UK carries unnecessary risks'. He cautioned that many current projects were 'hanging on a knife edge' and that 'expansion which would normally have come to the UK is being re-evaluated for exchange rate reasons'.[13]

Inward investors themselves have taken the unusual step of publicly voicing the same concerns. Kunio Nakamura, global president of Matsushita, the world's largest consumer electronics manufacturer, encapsulated their feelings when he said that 'a strong pound is making it difficult for us to continue production in the country' and 'if Britain does nothing to solve the problem, foreign companies, regardless of whether they are Japanese, American or whatever nationality, may exit the country'.[14] Some have already started opening new plants in the euro-zone rather than in Britain, and others have even closed existing factories here to relocate there. In just a few weeks in South Wales alone, Hitachi axed 350 staff in Hirwaun, Sony cut 400 jobs at Pencoed and Panasonic laid off 1,300 workers in Cardiff; each one blamed currency instability.

The opportunity to prise inward investors away from Britain is being seized by Ireland. In a blatant pitch, promotional material from the local Industrial Development Agency temptingly observes that 'Ireland, as one of the founder members of the EMU and the only English speaking one, can offer significant advantages to companies locating here. These advantages include the elimination of exchange rate risks and transaction costs, consistently lower interest rates and a generally more predictable economic environment in which to operate.'[15]

The ploy has been working. Britain still tops the inward investment league tables in the EU because most current schemes were initiated three or four years ago and most inward investors still assume Britain will join the euro at some point. But in 1999 our share of the new projects in Europe slipped from 28 per cent to 24 per cent, while the French share jumped from 12 per cent to 18 per cent, as inward investment rose by 11 per cent in the euro-zone but fell by 18 per cent in countries outside.[16] If we rejected the single currency once and for all, or even continued to postpone the decision, our share would undoubtedly plummet as it did when we were locked out of the Common Market.

The most high-profile casualty has been motor manufacturing. Britain has paid a uniquely high price for the worldwide overproduction of cars because outside the single currency we are easy prey for cuts in capacity. The US firm Ford lost more than £120 million in 1999 from its British operations and in 2000 it announced that production at Dagenham is to be ended after sixty-nine years, with the loss of 3,250 jobs, as the Fiesta moves to Cologne. 'If you don't have any sterling exposure, if you're entirely euro-based, you've had something close to a 30 per cent advantage over those people who are manufacturing vehicles in this country,' complained Nick Scheele, chairman of Ford Europe.[17] Vauxhall, owned by the US giant General Motors, spent £10 million in 1999 on transaction and hedging costs and in 2000 it announced that 2,200 jobs will go when its Luton plant closes. 'Our view as a company is that we'd like to get into the euro as soon as possible,' implored Nick Reilly, chairman and chief executive of Vauxhall in Britain.[18]

The Japanese companies Honda, Toyota and Nissan are set to become Britain's largest car manufacturers, having together invested £4.5 billion here. But neither Honda nor Toyota have made a profit in the past few years while Carlos Ghosn, global president of Nissan, reflected that 'it was practically impossible to make a profit in 2000 if you were not manufacturing in euro'.[19] Nissan established its Sunderland factory in 1984, rejuvenating a region devastated by the collapse of traditional manufacturing. Although it is the most efficient car plant in Europe, it endured months of speculation that it might be forced to close because of the high pound, and was in the end saved not least because the EU approved emergency aid of £40 million amid rumours that the government had privately indicated its intention to join the euro. It is not known if promises were made, but it is apparent that assumptions have been made. Referring to future investment decisions, Ghosn asked 'Why do you want to take a currency risk with the pound if you have the possibility of being risk-free in the euro?'[20]

In addition to foreign businesses, British multinationals with factories across Europe have also found it increasingly difficult to justify investment here over the euro-zone. Some have been shifting production abroad, as Nestlé has been slowly moving KitKat from York to Hamburg. 'In today's increasingly international economy our factories are not just in competition with other food companies. They are also in competition with each other,' said Peter Blackburn, chairman and chief executive of Nestlé in Britain. Citing the added costs caused by the high pound, he noted that 'Nestlé has not lost sales. Production has simply transferred from our factories in the UK to our factories elsewhere in Europe.'[21]

### Jobs

The overall strength of the British economy has brought unemployment down to its lowest level for a generation. This performance would have been even better, however, but for sterling seesawing in value: hundreds of companies publicly quoted the high pound as wholly or partially responsible when between them they cut a total of 11,000 jobs in 1999 and 41,000 jobs in 2000.[22]

On top of these 52,000, there was a knock-on effect down the supply chain. Using the rule of thumb that for every job directly dependent on trade with the EU there are a further 0.6 jobs indirectly linked, it is possible to infer that another 31,000 jobs were destroyed.[23] This means that since the launch of the euro Britain has been shedding an average of 3,500 jobs per month.

As each person out of work costs an average of £12,000

in extra benefits and lost taxes, unemployment due to the high pound could have potentially burdened working people to the tune of £1 billion in two years.[24] Of course, if our economy had been weaker, or if we had ruled out for certain the prospect of joining the euro, the damage would have been even worse and those losing their jobs would have found it harder to get new work.

Even when sterling finally recedes against the euro and the problems of the high pound ebb away, the lessons of history and economics are that they will return. If the sterling–euro relationship settles at equilibrium for some time, exchange rate risks will not have disappeared because it is the possibility of future disequilibrium that is the fundamental threat. In other words, the recent trouble of the high pound is just a case study, the latest manifestation of the inevitable and increasing volatility of sterling.

### Prices and mortgages

Prices of the same goods and services vary considerably throughout Europe. As shown by the tabloid 'rip-off Britain' campaign and the queues of British shoppers nipping across the Channel to stock up in foreign supermarkets, we suffer particularly badly. The European Consumers' Organisation showed when the euro was launched that Britain was the most expensive country in Europe, particularly for popular consumer durables, with prices up to 17 per cent higher than in France and 24 per cent more than in Germany.[25] The British Consumers' Association revealed that by the end of 2000 famous brands – like Chanel No. 5 perfume, Levi jeans and Sony PlayStation – were 20 per cent more expensive in Britain than elsewhere in Europe.[26] Another survey, for *The Sunday Times*, exposed that an identical basket of groceries costs £40 in Britain but about £6 less in France and Germany.[27]

Although there are many reasons for this, a central factor has been the ability of firms to charge different prices in different currencies because consumers have been unable to shop around to get the best deals. Such huge disparities do not exist in the United States because its common charging system drives all prices down towards the least expensive markets as transparency exposes extortionate sellers. 'With a single currency, prices in one EU state will be directly comparable with prices in another,' the British Consumers' Association has noted; 'this should enhance competition and ensure that consumers enjoy wider choice and keener prices'.[28] In the short term Britain will not benefit from downward pressure on prices as currency fluctuations make bills harder to compare. In the long term our prices might even rise as businesses that are forced to offer reductions elsewhere in Europe can get away with making their products more expensive in Britain to compensate for lost profits.

The ambition of stable prices is at the core of Economic and Monetary Union. The Maastricht criteria for applicants, endorsed by the Stability and Growth Pact that members must sign, have already cut public borrowing throughout the euro-zone; and the European Central Bank has a strict inflation target of less than 2 per cent, regardless of the electoral cycles that have so often enticed British governments to go for broke in an effort to win votes. Although the Bank of England has now been given the independence to set interest rates to meet its own inflation target, there is no guarantee that in future a less prudent and more desperate government might not claw that power back.

History shows that the Europeans have a far better record

than we do. Since 1960 inflation has averaged 6.9 per cent in Britain but only 3.4 per cent in Germany. This explains the significant interest rate differential. Since 1950 interest rates have oscillated wildly but averaged 7.5 per cent in Britain compared to a more even 5.1 per cent in Germany. The European apparatus will almost certainly bring about limited prospects for boom and bust as well as entrenching lower inflation and lower interest rates.

Regardless of our own ability to end boom and bust and control inflation, Britain is likely to suffer higher interest rates than if we were in the single currency. This is because investors holding sterling assets are bound to demand bigger returns to compensate for the unique exchange rate risks that they will face. This in turn means that homeowners would not be able to unlock lower mortgage payments. The Council of Mortgage Lenders has accepted that 'it is conventional wisdom that interest rates under the ECB will be lower and more stable than if the UK stayed outside'.[29] And the editor of *Your Mortgage* magazine has consequently observed that 'if the UK joins the euro it will mean a massive cut in Middle Britain's mortgage bills'.[30]

Joining the euro is the logical extension of a process begun when we finally entered Europe in 1973, and rejecting it would be tantamount to reversing nearly thirty years of policy devoted to free trade, dynamic innovation and wealth creation. Britain is an island trading nation so stability in our trading relations with our biggest trading partners is unusually central to our national prosperity. The entire history of our involvement in Europe has been about promoting free trade and entrenching trading stability. From the beginning the Treaty of Rome minimised tariffs between members to forge a Common Market. The Single European Act extended the objective by overhauling regulations to create a Single Market. The Maastricht Treaty was designed to complete the picture by removing exchange rate hurdles.

Erratic currencies are just as much a barrier to trade as tariffs and regulations because of the uncertainty they inject into business planning. In staying out in the long term we would effectively be cutting ourselves off from equal access to the enlarged internal market we have worked so hard to build. This would undoubtedly hit our exports, our inward investment, our jobs and our standard of living, while injecting a dangerous element of permanent instability into our economy.

We would also miss out on new opportunities available to our leading competitors, and not only cheaper prices and mortgages. British enterprises would struggle to take advantage of the larger economies of scale and greater investment potential open to European firms. Any European company with revenue streams in several different currencies used to have a strong incentive to maintain some production in each country as a natural hedge against exchange rate movements; unlike its rivals in the US, it could not design its structures on a least-cost basis across a wide area without exchange rate risks. That is no longer true: the advent of the euro has already sparked an outbreak of restructuring, mergers, acquisitions and joint ventures, a trend that is sure to continue as national players seek pan-European reach and improved competitiveness. In addition, most financial investment in Europe used to be in the domestic economy, with many insurance companies and pension funds obliged to minimise their risks by holding significant proportions of their assets in the same currency as their liabilities. Those requirements are relaxing too: under the euro businesses will be able to raise capital across the Continent, attracting investors looking for the highest possible returns.

Quite simply, if Britain joins the euro in the right conditions then we would all be better off than if we stay outside. One of the most important academic studies in this field has shown that the single currency might boost trade within the EU by up to 50 per cent; if Britain were to join it would mean roughly 6 per cent more of our output would be exported and 6 per cent more of our expenditure imported.[31] This would have a significant impact on our growth trends. Lehman Brothers forecasts that if we were in the euro in 2003 then our growth would be 2.8 per cent against 2.7 per cent if we were outside, and by 2004 it would be 3.1 per cent rather than 2.6 per cent.[32] Because of the direct link between trade, growth and wealth, this would substantially improve our prosperity. Goldman Sachs predicts that it would probably increase our income per head by as much as 3 per cent.[33] These are considerable benefits to forgo for the sake of political dogma.

By denying ourselves a level playing field, staying out would clearly mean losing out. Actively choosing not to join, or even continuing to defer a conscious decision, would certainly lead to more high-profile casualties. But it is unlikely that there would be a sudden economic disaster, a massive collapse in trade or a huge hike in unemployment. Although some sectors would obviously suffer immediately, especially in manufacturing, for a few years our economy might be able to carry on as if little had changed. Gradually, however, perhaps almost imperceptibly, we would fail to fulfil our economic potential and start to slip behind our European rivals, with slower growth rates than theirs and more job losses than we would otherwise have had. After all, we have been in that boat before: it is exactly what happened when we spurned the ECSC and the EEC until harsh reality finally drove us in.

## Arguments against joining

Although the case for Britain joining the single currency is extremely powerful, a balanced judgement must also consider the arguments against. Opponents usually emphasise political issues, but about the economics they make one serious charge: that an interest rate set for the entire euro-zone might not always be appropriate for Britain. This is a material question that must be properly addressed. However, the more zealous antagonists do themselves a disservice by embellishing their case with a host of silly or frankly irrelevant points.[34]

### The euro will collapse
From the beginning, some have argued that Britain should not bother worrying about Economic and Monetary Union because it would never get off the ground. Mimicking those who predicted that Schuman and Messina would not come to anything, they repeatedly forecast that EMU would not see the light of day. For instance, when Margaret Thatcher was asked in 1988 about the chances of the Delors Report paving the way for a European Central Bank, she replied 'I neither want nor expect to see in my lifetime, nor indeed, twanging my harp, after my lifetime, such an institution.'[35]

'I do not believe monetary union is achievable,' averred Norman Lamont in 1995. 'For me, the real danger about monetary union is not that it will happen. Rather it is that another attempt, doomed to failure, will be made.'[36] 'It is a fantasy and it is just not going to happen,' confirmed Tim Congdon, a hostile economist, in 1996. 'Neither the EU nor a subset of its members will have a single currency on January 1 1999, January 1 2002, January 1 2003, or, indeed, at any date in the relevant future.'[37]

Like Marxists constantly predicting the inevitable collapse of capitalism, they have been proved wrong. The period of greatest potential danger, between setting entry exchange rates in May 1998 and locking values in January 1999, a time of global financial instability, passed without hitch. Reality has confounded wishful thinking, and soothsaying that the euro will be destroyed and replaced by its original constituent currencies is heard less and less these days.

### Transition costs

If we were ever to consider joining, opponents say, the transition costs would prove prohibitively expensive. A report for Business for Sterling maintained that they would come to as much as £36 billion.[38] Although this figure has been widely ridiculed – it was even disowned by Francis Maude – transferring from one currency to another would undoubtedly require investment in new Automated Teller Machines, cash tills, computer software and so on, just as it did when Britain decimalised in 1971.

A survey by Andersen Consulting showed that for four-fifths of firms the cost of this changeover would be less than 0.5 per cent of turnover.[39] Estimates in the twelve countries that have already adopted the euro suggest that their total costs have been below 0.5 per cent of GDP.[40] This is the same proportion that the CBI calculates it would be for Britain, about £4.5 billion.[41] Of the reputable calculations, Bannock

Consulting predicts that at the very most it could cost
Britain is £11.7 billion.[42]

Much of this investment would in any case not be additional, it would simply need to be brought forward: younger
generations of ATMs and cash tills are constantly being
introduced and companies frequently modernise their IT
infrastructure, so Britain could almost transfer by truncating
the life cycle of planned spending. Sensible businesses are
rightly bracing themselves for the euro whether we join or
not, so they are currently making the relevant investment
anyway. For example, Boots has spent £7 million preparing
to use the euro in the rest of its European markets and only
a proportion of that would be needed to bring their operations in Britain up to scratch, and the Automatic Vending
Association estimates that its members are investing £100
million to allow British vending machines to accept euros as
well as pounds.

Peter Williams, chairman of the British Retail Consor-
tium's single currency committee, predicts that widespread
use of euro cash in British shops 'will be started by foreign
tourists bringing in the new currency, but more and more
British businessmen working in Europe and Britons return-
ing from holiday will start contributing too'.[43] That is why
retailers like Dixons, Harrods, Marks & Spencer, Selfridges
and Virgin have already made the investment necessary to
allow euro notes and coins to be taken in their shops in
Britain from January 2002.

High street banks, including Abbey National and Barclays,
already offer financial products denominated in euros, rang-
ing from current accounts to mortgages. Supermarkets like
Asda and Sainsbury's, and DIY stores such as B&Q, have
already introduced trolleys that use euros as well as pounds,

British Telecom is preparing its phone boxes to accept euros, and euros will be taken in some NCP car parks as well. British business is preparing for the euro regardless of whether we are in the single currency, so it is already absorbing some of the transition costs without accessing all the benefits.

In any case, the one-off transition costs would be more than offset by the ongoing savings from eliminating transaction costs, the commission fees and administration charges paid just to change money. Britons make about 35 million journeys to the European Union each year, nearly three times more trips than to the rest of the world, and every traveller loses money when converting pounds into euros. According to the CBI, Britons on holiday and on business would save a total of 0.4 per cent of GDP or £3.6 billion a year – that is £170 a year for every household in the country – merely from abolishing these transaction costs.[44] Without even taking account of the savings that would flow from the end of exchange rate risks, in two or three years this alone would repay the transition costs if they were anything like those for the current members.

### Internet trading

One of the more fanciful suggestions is that the growing popularity of internet trading will somehow allow online purchases to circumvent currency fluctuations, rendering Economic and Monetary Union what opponents like to call an out-of-date response to an old-fashioned problem. This argument, such as it is, was central to a report on reasons to 'Keep the Pound' commissioned by the Tory Party, in which the former Conservative Cabinet Minister John Nott claimed that 'the internet inhabits a borderless world where trading and currency blocs are irrelevant'.[45] Really? Business for Sterling has devoted an entire pamphlet to this bizarre proposition.[46] And Janet Bush, director of New Europe, has said that 'currencies are increasingly irrelevant. I think in ten years' time there will be a single world currency, and it will be electronic, it will be on the internet.'[47]

What is missing from this odd chain of reasoning is that no matter which medium facilitates purchases – be it in cash or on credit – they still need to be paid for. If that involves spending one currency for an item priced in another then it will be subject to both transaction costs and exchange rate risks, just like any other kind of trade. In fact, far from the internet making the single currency redundant, because the euro removes these barriers then if we join it is likely to promote the more rapid spread of e-commerce in Britain and Europe.

### Unfunded pensions

Those who are ideologically hostile to the euro, and therefore unwilling to examine honestly its pros and cons, allege that if we joined then Britons would end up paying for the pension liabilities of other EU members. This is what Nott, in his report for Hague, called 'the smoking time bomb [sic] of unfunded pensions'.[48] It is a much-repeated calumny.

Many Continental countries provide their pensions out of current revenue rather than accumulated capital, just as we pay for our National Health Service. As the population ages then it is true that all these costs are likely to rise unless action is taken. But it is not true that if either their pensions or our NHS went bust, any other country would pick up the tab. This possibility is specifically excluded under Article 104 of the Maastricht Treaty, the so-called no-bail-out clause, which clearly says that 'a Member State shall not be liable for or assume the commitments of central governments, regional, local or other public authorities, other bodies governed by public law or public undertakings of another Member State'. End of story.

## Taxation and unemployment

A common scare story is that if we joined the euro then British taxes would be harmonised, which is code for increased. Another is that European unemployment levels would be imported, raising our jobless figures. The underlying allegation is that the Continent suffers from a supposedly sclerotic social model that we would somehow be forced to adopt, undoing our liberal reforms and hampering the competitiveness of our economy.

Yet the single currency is a monetary not a fiscal measure, not directly connected to taxation. Therefore, those who genuinely believe that the European Commission is bent on putting up our taxes have no defence in merely dodging the euro; their only recourse must be to escape from the EU altogether. But they are wrong. It is perfectly possible for nations in the euro-zone to tax and spend as much or as little as they like, so long as they do not slump into heavy debt. For example, in France public spending comes to more than half of GDP while in Ireland it is less than a third, so the two governments need very different levels of taxation to balance their books, a judgement over which the Commission has no say.

Perhaps it is not surprising that tax scares, the meat and drink of electoral over-hype, are treated seriously. After all, in signing the Single European Act Margaret Thatcher established the principle that the Commission can make minor proposals on indirect taxation, such as VAT and excise duties.

And it is true that some countries would like the Commission to have greater powers, a point that anti-Europeans repeat until they are blue in the face.

But the EU can only express a view on tax where it relates to the functioning of the internal market or on environmental grounds. Even in these areas Britain has a right of veto. Income tax and corporation tax are matters for national governments alone and beyond the reach of the EU. Britain can also veto any attempt to remove our veto on tax or any other matters. So there is no prospect whatsoever that taxes could be harmonised or increased without prior British consent, whatever others may want.

In any case, the European consensus has moved away from tax harmonisation. When William Hague and Michael Portillo alleged during the 2001 election campaign that Brussels had secret plans to harmonise income taxes and corporation taxes, the Commission rejected the accusation out of hand. Far from proposing further tax harmonisation it actually favours greater tax competition. 'A reasonable degree of tax competition within the EU is healthy,' its policy statement says. 'Tax competition may strengthen fiscal discipline to the extent that it encourages Member States to streamline their public expenditure, thus allowing a reduction in the overall tax burden.' It asserts that 'Member States are free to choose the structures of their tax systems as well as the tax rates and tax bases that they consider most appropriate and according to their preferences,' concluding that 'it is clear that there is no need for an across the board harmonisation of Member States' tax systems'.[49]

Similarly, it is irresponsible for scaremongers to pretend that embracing a single currency also entails accepting higher unemployment levels or common industrial policies. It does not. In so far as Britain has more people in work or is more competitive than some European economies, that is to our advantage as long as we are allowed to compete on equal terms and are not held back by self-inflicted currency barriers. Neither unemployment nor industrial policies can leak across the Channel. In any case, most of the EU is more prosperous and more productive than we are, and the reform effort is bringing down taxation and unemployment, just as it is instilling supply side flexibility, not least because of incentives generated by the single currency itself.

### 'One size fits all' interest rate

Apart from these points there is one important accusation levelled against Economic and Monetary Union: that because the European Central Bank determines monetary policy to suit the euro-zone as a whole, not the specific needs of the British economy, if we joined then we might end up with an interest rate inappropriate for our economic situation. This is a rather more salient concern, causing reasonable people pause for thought, that requires detailed consideration.

No interest rate would ever be ideal for all parts of Britain, whether it is set in London or elsewhere. Different sectors and different regions usually require different interest rates. This problem was highlighted in 1991 by Norman Lamont, the Chancellor, and in 1998 by Eddie George, the governor of the Bank of England, who both sought to justify their interest rates – which were thought too high in the depressed north but ideal for the roaring south – by arguing that northern unemployment was 'a price well worth paying' to contain southern inflation. Sluggish growth in manufacturing has often cried out for a low rate while rapid expansion of services augured for a high one. In fact, parts of northern England, Wales and Scotland have far more in common with the economies of manufacturing regions across Europe than they do with London and the South East.

The interest rate is always a compromise between competing needs. In this respect, it should be noted that if Britain did join the euro-zone then we would be its second or third largest economy, more or less equal to France and just behind Germany, so we would be a substantial player with real pull over the ECB.

The United States shows that it is possible for a vast area to function effectively with a common monetary policy, even when parts of the economy are growing at separate speeds. The chances of the interest rate requirements of any area diverging from the rest are smaller in the euro-zone than in the US, as European countries are less economically specialised than American states and therefore less likely to be seriously out of kilter with each other. There is no European equivalent to Texas, for instance, which is totally dependent on oil, so economic shocks affecting only one EU country are extremely rare.

That is not to deny that Britain or any other member could be hit by a shock unique to it, thus requiring specific policy responses. In those circumstances, as Wim Duisenberg acknowledged in his president's foreword to the first annual report of the ECB, national governments must take action to deal with the problem. 'In any monetary union of the size of the euro area it is inevitable that inflation and other economic developments will not be completely uniform across all the countries involved,' he wrote. 'The existence of such differences, unless they exceed certain levels, should be seen as normal, as shown by the experience in other large monetary unions, such as the United States. However, should differences threaten to become too large, the policy response can only be provided nationally.'[50]

National governments in the euro-zone are still able to change fiscal policy to offset shocks. In any case, when demand falls the automatic stabilisers kick in: more is paid out in benefits and less is collected in taxes, so the budget deficit increases, which is permissible as long as it is not excessive. This is not what happens in the United States, where most states are legally obliged to balance their budgets every year, so when a state suffers a unique shock, it is the federal government that has to cushion the blow through transfer payments and the social security system. This explains why opponents of the euro are wrong to pretend the single currency requires increased or vastly harmonised taxes and wrong to allege it will need a huge rise in the central EU budget to fund a mechanism of counter-cyclical payments. The fact is that unlike American states European governments can still make regional grants to poor areas without reference to a central agency, so the EU budget need not increase from its present tight limit of 1.27 per cent of GNP and it could not do so anyway without the unanimous agreement of members.

Market flexibility, especially for labour, is also critical to allow a huge single currency area to cope with differing rates of growth. Theory dictates that any negative shock should cut wages to maintain employment levels; it also says that people made redundant should move to find jobs elsewhere. Thanks to recent reforms, wages are becoming more elastic in Europe, but it is true that levels of migration are lower in the communities of Europe than across the US with its frontier culture. Not only are Europeans deterred from moving between countries, because of linguistic and cultural differences as well as traditional currency barriers, but we move less readily within countries too. Hence there are black spots of regional unemployment. This problem has been offset in recent years by the faster mobility of capital. These days, factories will open in poor areas as long as there is a large pool of skilled labour, which is often cheaper than in rich areas. That is why inward investment has flooded into places like the North East, South Wales and Central Scotland.

Given these available instruments, there is no reason why Britain or any other member of the single currency should not be able to cope with any local shocks, despite losing control of interest rates. Yet to substantiate their worries, opponents of the euro point to Ireland during 2000, where overheating required a high interest rate but slower growth in the rest of the euro-zone meant it got a low one. In fact, Ireland decided that the long-term gains of joining the single currency out of synch with other members – such as demonstrating their pro-European credentials to potential inward investors – outweighed any short-term costs. By insisting on meeting Gordon Brown's five economic tests, Britain is in a totally different position. These tests demand sufficiently close convergence between the economic cycles before we enter, effectively requiring the euro-zone interest rate to be near a level that we would have chosen anyway.

Opponents argue that this convergence is unlikely because our economic cycles are inherently more compatible with the US than with Europe. That has been true since the end of the 1980s, when the Lawson boom-bust and German reunification conspired to decouple the similar cycles that Britain and Europe had enjoyed since the Second World War. There is considerable evidence, however, that our economies are beginning to converge again now. A flood of reports from respected bodies has recently suggested that all the indicators, except the aberrant exchange rate, are once more becoming aligned, not just temporarily but over the long term.[51] Given the little likelihood of Britain suffering from an inappropriate level of interest rate for our needs, and the considerable power at our command to deal with that eventuality should it arise, the risks from joining are therefore minor.

It is easy to understand the concerns of those who at first glance are wary of the complex economics of the single currency. But the risks tend to be exaggerated by opponents who have a political agenda, and in any case the potential problems can be solved by the proper use of domestic policy levers. Against that must be weighed the benefits that are there for the taking if we joined, as well as the dangers of staying outside: the missed opportunities that would hold us back and the damage that is likely to be done to our exports, our inward investment and our jobs. The choice is therefore not, as some like to pretend, between a leap in the dark and the security of the world we have known before.

A Canadian economist, Robert Mundell, first advanced the theory of optimum currency areas as long ago as 1961.[52] He demonstrated then that the ideal size of an economy with just one currency reflects the balance between the potential for independent interest rates to deal with changes in demand (suggesting a smaller area) against the danger that currency volatility will itself induce economic damage (calling for a larger one). The fact of the matter is that with the high level of British dependence on foreign trade, since the advent of globalisation and the launch of the euro as a response to it by the majority of our closest and biggest trading partners, as Mundell himself has concluded, this calculation has shifted decisively in favour of an area far larger than Britain. On balance, the pragmatic conclusion has to be that our economy has much more to gain than lose by entering. So businesses and the government should make preparations, and as soon as the Chancellor's five tests have been met we should agree to sign up. That means winning a Yes vote in a referendum.

# Britain's National Interests

## British sovereignty

Fear has dominated the debate about Europe in Britain for fifty years; for a small but influential minority who are significantly overrepresented in the public debate, alarm has boiled into anger, reaching hysteria against the single currency. The balance of economic evidence points in favour of joining when the conditions are right, but this reasonable judgement has been lost in a swirling miasma of dread panic whipped up in the media about the political implications. At the heart of these objections seems to be an almost visceral belief in the sanctity of national sovereignty, which has been wrongly equated with national preservation.

The argument for 'pooling' sovereignty was originally made by Winston Churchill, the embodiment of Great Power Britishness, who succinctly called for 'some sacrifice or merger of national sovereignty'. He explained that 'it is also possible and not less agreeable to regard it as the gradual assumption, by all nations concerned, of that larger sovereignty which can also protect their diverse and distinctive customs and characteristics, and their national traditions'.[1] This is the touchstone of the case for Britain in Europe and Britain in the euro.

### Parliamentary sovereignty

Britain's sovereign authority, the King or Queen in Parliament, was identified in the Bill of Rights of 1689, which confirmed the principle that monarchs are not above the law. That constitutional settlement evolved into the doctrine of 'parliamentary sovereignty', elaborated by A.V. Dicey in the *Law of the Constitution* in 1885, which asserted that only parliament has 'the right to make or unmake any law whatever'. Save New Zealand, Britain is unique in adhering to what Dicey called the 'absolute omnipotence' of parliament, as all other democracies have either federal divisions of authority or other written constitutions that restrict parliamentary supremacy to prevent the violation of fundamental rights and freedoms.

This concept of parliamentary sovereignty was challenged by the prospect of entering the European Economic Community. Passing the European Communities Bill involved a 'constitutional innovation', as the Lord Chancellor put it, through 'the acceptance in advance as part of the law of the United Kingdom of provisions to be made in the future by instruments issued by the Community institutions'.[2] As Britain was to be only one of nine members of the EEC, parliament was voluntarily admitting the joint authority of the other eight over aspects of its dominion.

The anti-Marketeers were enraged. Enoch Powell declared that he was not elected 'a member of our sovereign parliament in order to consent to that sovereignty being abated or transferred' and that he did not believe people would tolerate 'sovereignty being abolished or transformed'.[3] Tony Benn told the Commons that 'If ever this House were to create a situation in which people thought that it no longer reflected their power ultimately to decide, I believe that parliamentary democracy, which hangs by a gossamer thread, could easily fall to the ground.'[4]

Yet parliament's ability to exercise its sovereignty had already been dramatically circumscribed. Britain accepted that reality, unpleasant though it was to many, in its most fundamental form in 1949 when we admitted that alone parliament could no longer even secure the defence of the realm, which is why we joined the NATO alliance.[5] Parliament on its own cannot combat modern threats like cross-border crime and terrorism, our economy is influenced by international finance and multinational corporations that are beyond government control, our culture is affected by mass communications from abroad and our environment is dirtied by filthy factories and deforestation across the world. Only Robinson Crusoe was effectively sovereign over all he surveyed, but now no country is a hermetically sealed island.

The discrepancy that has emerged between parliament's unlimited theoretical authority and its restricted effective power is the nub of the issue. For legal authority is a necessary but insufficient condition for a state to protect the security and nurture the prosperity of its citizens. It also needs the practical power to implement its will. These days individual states by themselves often cannot discipline, let alone shape, international forces. To heighten their power and regain a degree of influence over events that affect them, they are therefore increasingly sharing with each other the exercise of aspects of their sovereignty. It is happening not just in NATO but also to varying degrees in regional blocs across the world, including NAFTA in North America, MERCOSUR in South America, ASEAN in Asia and of course in the European Union.

This is the *casus belli* of most of those hostile to the euro. But in defending the legal concept of parliamentary sovereignty, anti-Europeans are in fact at odds with their own heroine. For the adoption of the single currency would involve no constitutional principles not already accepted by Margaret Thatcher when she signed the Single European Act, which granted a legislative function to the European Parliament and abolished the national veto in many policy areas.[6] This explains why many of those agitating against Britain's entry into the euro are logically and in truth opposed to Britain's place in Europe.

### Pooled sovereignty

If the notion of absolutely omnipotent parliamentary sovereignty has become a poor guide to exercising authority, it makes sense to formulate a concept relevant to the modern world. This, after all, is in the classic tradition of British constitutional evolution, which has repeatedly modified its theories by pragmatic convention in the light of changed circumstances; there is something rather un-British about attempts by Powell, Benn and others to posit an immutable constitutional apparatus for all time.

The power of a sovereign authority is properly described by its ability to work for what it believes to be in the national interest. So effective sovereignty is best defined as the practical capacity of a state to maximise its influence on behalf of its citizens, to advance their interests.

By using a formulation like this, appreciation of how a nation might choose to deploy its sovereignty is transformed. There is no longer a zero-sum game where sovereignty is either safeguarded or forfeited; it can be exercised in concert or 'pooled' with other sovereign states. This is precisely what happens through the European Union where members exchange the authority of solitary decision-making – in restricted amounts and in limited areas – to win the increased power of decisions taken by fifteen states. Choosing to exercise legal sovereignty collectively therefore amounts to a larger effective sovereignty, exactly as Churchill described.

This partnership can be illustrated by the analogy of a rope.[7] Each of the fifteen members, with their own national identities, is symbolised by a different-coloured skein of silk; braided together they retain their individuality, distinct enough to be seen separately one from another, but gather in strength. This thought is at the very heart of the Treaty of Rome, in which the phrase 'ever closer union' implies proximity not merger, with members discrete as well as integrated.

Contrary to the accusations of contemporary anti-Europeans who claim to have been duped in the past, this argument has been made forcefully each time Britain has considered European integration. 'Talk about loss of sovereignty becomes all the more meaningless when one remembers that practically every nation, including our own, has already been forced by the pressures of the modern world to abandon large areas of sovereignty and to realise that we are now all inter-dependent,' wrote Harold Macmillan to explain the reasons for his application for membership as long ago as 1961. 'No country today, not even the giants of

America or Russia, can pursue purely independent policies in defence, foreign affairs or the economic sphere.'[8]

In support of Edward Heath's negotiations in 1971, the Government published a White Paper that noted 'there is no question of any erosion of essential national sovereignty; what is proposed is a sharing and an enlargement of individual national sovereignties in the general interest'. Without which, it went on, 'our power to influence the Communities would steadily diminish, while the Communities' power to affect our future would as steadily increase'.[9] During the 1975 referendum campaign, Margaret Thatcher agreed. 'Britain has for generations thought of herself as a power that was different in kind. Proudly so. It is this sense of distinctiveness that anti-marketeers play upon when they promise "independence" by return of post,' she said, 'but their prospectus ignores the fact that almost every major nation has been obliged by the pressures of the post-war world to pool significant areas of sovereignty so as to create more effective political units.'[10]

It is this very point that now underpins the argument for joining the single currency. We can no longer ensure our economic stability or eradicate the damaging effects of currency volatility without working closely with our biggest trading partners. But, as any agreement voluntarily entered can be unilaterally revoked, parliament and the people retain the right to rescind all previous decisions, including those to join the EU or the euro. That remains the ultimate guarantor of national sovereignty.

## United Europe of States

The European Union is founded on agreement between proud nations that have voluntarily pooled aspects of their sovereignty. Anti-Europeans have claimed for many years that this process has gone too far and that joining the single currency would be tantamount to surrendering control over our own affairs. To substantiate this allegation they highlight remarks by European leaders calling for greater integration.

The truth is that because the EU is gradually evolving without a set plan there is a constant debate about its future direction. And although some federalist voices can be heard, almost nobody of significance has ever called for the submersion of national identity in a central 'superstate'. We have repeatedly excluded ourselves from these discussions by allowing our anxieties over sovereignty to paralyse our response to others' initiatives. For the same reason, it is very rare that we have led developments from the front. But as we simply cannot avoid the consequences of decisions taken on the Continent, it is obviously in our own national interests to maximise our influence over them.

### Superstate, no

European centralists and anti-Europeans are agreed that Britain has no chance of leading in Europe because the process of integration is a never-ending treadmill to what they call a 'superstate'. This underpins their shared belief that Britain's national identity is under threat. But in their wild dreams the centralists have done nothing more than erect a straw doll for the antis to knock down.

'Let's be clear,' said Romano Prodi, president of the Commission, 'I do not want Europe to become a "superstate".'[11]

It could not be clearer. Unsurprisingly, there is no demand for a 'superstate' from any head of government in Europe either, not least because all of them cherish their national identities as much as we do ours. 'It cannot be the goal of European policy to establish a European central state, that is to say, a centrally structured Europe,' the French President and the German Chancellor wrote in a joint letter to Tony Blair in 1998; 'we must rather do all we can to create a strong European Union with the necessary scope for action and the capacity to preserve and foster the diversity and richness of Europe's political, cultural and regional traditions.'[12]

Few countries on earth are as protective of their national identity as France, and it beggars belief that the French would ever allow their nationhood to be robbed by a 'super-state'. While France has recently been in the vanguard for further integration, this is certainly not at the expense of Frenchness. Jacques Chirac, the President, told the Bundestag in 2000 that 'it's misrepresenting the truth to say that, on one side, there are those who are defending national sovereignty and, on the other, those who are selling it off. Neither you nor we are envisaging the creation of a super European state which would supplant our national states and mark the end of their existence as players in international life,' because 'our nations are the source of our identities and our roots' and 'nations will remain the first reference points'.[13]

It is true that there are federalists currently in senior positions in Germany – that has been the case for forty years – but they too oppose a 'superstate'. What they want in fact is greater powers for the regions, an important political con-stituency in Germany. Joschka Fischer, the Foreign Minister and leading federalist, regularly condemns centralisation. 'The nightmare of British eurosceptics, the so-called "super-

state", a new sovereign that would abolish the old nation
states along with their democratic governments is,' he told a
British audience in 2001, 'nothing but a synthetic construct
which has nothing whatsoever to do with European reality.'[14]

If the EU really were driving towards a 'superstate' it must
mean that proud nations like France and Germany are either
content to see their independence destroyed or have not
noticed it is happening. And it would make it astonishing
that countries like Estonia, Latvia and Lithuania – nations
that existed only in the mind a decade ago, whose identities
have recently become visible for the first time in over half a
century – are queuing up to join in.

The whole idea of a 'superstate' is nothing more than a
politically motivated hoax. Forty years of European integration have so far built a structure with an annual revenue of
about £60 billion, less than two-thirds the amount that
Britain spends every year on social security payments alone.
While it cannot rise above 1.27 per cent of European GNP
without the unanimous agreement of members, European
governments control an average of 44 per cent of their GDP.
How can the EU, with less than 3 per cent of the average
expenditure available to European governments, possibly be
a 'superstate'?

It is not, there is no serious demand for one, and there are
no suitable conditions for one. A 'superstate' would be
impossible without the majority of each country's people
becoming infused with a genuinely European consciousness
that transcended their loyalty to their nation. But there is no
European language, no European public and no European
consensus; in short, there is no European identity of a kind
that could conceivably facilitate the withering of national
loyalties.

Anti-Europeans accuse political leaders of trying to impose a European identity and a 'superstate' by means of the single currency. But this logic is flawed because the euro is primarily an economic measure. There are many examples in history of monetary unions that did not lead to political union, including those effectively between Britain and Ireland from 1921 to 1979 and Germany and the Netherlands since 1983.[15] The 'superstate' imagined by a small number of British European centralists and feared by various groups of British anti-Europeans is simply not on the cards.

### Power-sharing, yes

It has been very easy for anti-Europeans to stir fears of an emerging 'superstate', despite the evidence, largely because it is difficult for others to define exactly what the European Union is. Having rightly preferred an incremental approach to adopting a grand plan – which is in the British tradition – European institutions have gradually educed into a new kind of polity, an entity that is neither a state nor a federation. Moreover, it is still work in progress and the members are drawing the map at the same time as they are exploring the route.

Through the Treaty of Rome and subsequent amendments to it the fifteen members of the EU have freely chosen to delegate the exercise of some national authority to a series of supranational institutions with overlapping jurisdictions. The novel feature, which distinguishes the EU from NATO and other international organisations, is that some of its common decisions take the form of legislative instruments that are legally binding on all members.

This complex decision-making process has forged a complicated condominium, something more than a free trade area but much less than a so-called 'superstate', where in some fields sovereign authority rests solely with the member country and in others it has been pooled. Over some policies, such as agriculture, fisheries and trade, there is a formal intermingling of decision-making through the use of Qualified Majority Voting, while in others, such as defence, immigration and taxation, conclusions require the unanimous support of all members, granting them the right of veto. Further areas, notably criminal law, remain completely outside the competence of the EU.

Ultimately control of the EU rests with the member countries. They must each agree and ratify any changes to treaties, concluded at Inter-Governmental Conferences. They send prime ministers, ministers, commissioners and central bank governors to the various EU institutions, while their citizens directly elect Members of the European Parliament. They choose transnational appointments such as the presidents of the Commission and the Central Bank. And they directly manage more than 85 per cent of European spending. They share this control with each other, and, far from relinquishing it to a central agency, the trend has been to find ways of making it more democratic and transparent.

The EU is composed of fifteen states and is clearly not itself a state. Neither is it strictly federal, as such systems imply a state comprising a number of areas or regions each of which have separate institutions whose powers are legitimised in the federal constitution. In the EU each nation derives its power from its own constitution not from Brussels. While nations have volunteered to work together, subjecting themselves to joint authority in carefully circumscribed spheres, they have not created a federal state. They retain their original rights and of course they could choose to withdraw.

*National interests*

European diplomacy is frequently portrayed in Britain as a constant struggle to stave off the combined forces of fourteen other countries unified under French and German command. Bernard Connolly, a disillusioned former Commission civil servant, put this at its most crude in his book *The Rotten Heart of Europe*. 'The Franco-German axis *is* the Community,' he declaimed, 'and the role of the other members of the European Council is to give a ceremonial benediction to what the French and German leaders want to do.'[16] This is nonsense.

Although the partnership between France and Germany has been central to the development of the EU, they frequently have conflicting interests. As the virtually simultaneous appearance in spring 2001 of draft documents by the respective ruling socialist parties showed, they have never been as far apart as at present.[17] For example, France wants more money for the EU, not least for the CAP, while Germany wants a ceiling on central funding and fundamental restructuring of the CAP to bring down costs. And it is ridiculous to suggest that the other members have no independent interests of their own. It was clear that they do from how hard each country fought to have the weight of its QMV allocation increased by the Nice Treaty in 2000. The fifteen are all foreigners to each other, not one homogeneous unit, each as distinct from one another as they are from us, proud of their own identities and resolute in advancing their own interests.

The EU effectively provides a modern and peaceful forum for the battle of these competing national interests as well as a mechanism for delivering action on common objectives. On different issues the members form different

alliances, constantly turning a kaleidoscope of shifting pat-
terns of allegiance. Far from other countries ganging up on
Britain, we are usually in the majority. For example, in the
Council of Ministers during 1998 Germany was outvoted
eighteen times, Italy thirteen times, France five times and
Britain just twice. Rather than precipitating the demise of
national loyalties, the reality is that European integration has
actually accentuated national differences as its members fight
their national corners.[18]

Partly because of our particular political tradition – with a
winner-takes-all election system and an adversarial parliamentary process that tend to reduce the chances of coalition
governments and strengthen the authority of the executive,
as well as an independent civil service that does not initiate
legislation – Britain has not always fully understood the culture of European politics. Power sharing, compromising with
politicians of different ideologies, and dealing in foreign languages that define inflammatory words like 'federalism' in
ways that most of us would not, all make it difficult for
British leaders to negotiate in Europe. Yet if we played the
game better, we would win more often.

## Historic damage

The argument about sovereignty is not just dry constitutional theory. Our failure to grasp the realities of
contemporary international diplomacy has severely harmed
our country over the past fifty years in practical ways that
have reduced our influence and restricted our economic
potential. Consideration of sovereignty should force us to
reassess the choices we make for our country, deciding which

actions are actually in our national interests rather than simply shouting about British superiority.

Britain emerged from the Second World War the principal victor in Western Europe, and some British statesmen showed signs of understanding the need for pooled sovereignty and therefore of changing attitudes to the Continent. 'There can be no revival of Europe without a spiritually great Germany,' Winston Churchill beneficently announced in his famous Zurich speech of 1946, adding that only in partnership with Germany could 'France recover the moral and cultural leadership of Europe'.[19] Ernest Bevin, who aided Continental recovery by implementing the Marshall Plan in 1948, instructed parliament that 'the old-fashioned conception of the balance of power as an aim should be discarded' because 'no one disputes the idea of European unity'.[20] This understanding raised the prospect of Britain heading a European 'Third Force' to equal the United States and the Soviet Union. But this historic moment was soon thrown away by lesser leaders over their qualms about sovereignty.

Since then we have been unsure what we want from Europe, and this lack of a driving narrative has left us isolated and damaged. By failing to appreciate the advantages to Britain of pooling sovereignty with our European partners, we have suffered in the past; if we do not overcome our fears now then we risk our future too.

### Locked out

As soon as the Schuman Plan was published France and West Germany understood the potential of pooled sovereignty to increase their power. Each immediately established clear and consistent agendas. France's first priority was to contain

German power, its second to restore a sense of pride by influencing the configuration of Europe. The ambition of the newly created FRG is summarised in a famous dictum by the novelist Thomas Mann, to create 'a European Germany, not a German Europe'. British hesitation quickly showed them both that they no longer needed us to arbitrate between them, thus ceding control to a Franco-German vision that we have been trying to come to terms with ever since.

The dramatic possibilities of 1945 were cast aside in little more than a decade and Harold Macmillan was left to confess that 'For the first time since the Napoleonic era, the major continental powers are united in a positive economic grouping, with considerable political aspects, which, though not specifically directed against the United Kingdom, may have the effect of excluding us both from European markets and from consultation in European policy.'[21] The entire history of British diplomacy had been devoted to averting this spectre, which we finally brought upon ourselves.

Attitudes to national identity in France have long resembled those in Britain. The difference has been that from the beginning France was confident its national interests could best be advanced through Europe. As a founder member, without rivalry from Britain and with the whip hand over Germany, it was more or less able to mould Europe in its own image.

France insisted on the creation of the Common Agricultural Policy, which was introduced in the early 1960s primarily to the benefit of French farmers and largely at the expense of West German (and later British) taxpayers. When Harold Wilson published a White Paper on the merits of membership in 1967, it estimated that because of the CAP joining could push up food prices by 14 per cent and the cost of living by 3.5 per cent.[22] France secured another deal on funding that was very much to its own advantage in the late 1960s. The price of entry jumped again. Wilson produced another White Paper in 1970 that assessed the damage to be far higher than just three years before, predicting that food prices could rise by 26 per cent and the cost of living by 5 per cent, while the balance of payments burden could be more than £1 billion.[23] France then cajoled the Community into concluding the Common Fisheries Policy the moment talks were opened with Britain, Denmark, Ireland and Norway, all of which have long coastlines and large fish stocks.

Entry was worth the pain because of the boost to exports and growth. Yet almost every day that passed made Britain more desperate to get in but less able to get a good deal. Over years of paranoid protection of our supposedly absolute sovereignty, we suffered isolated decline. By the time we recognised reality in 1971, Britain was a supplicant forced to accept the entire *acquis communautaire*, the patrimony of principles, policies, practices, laws and obligations already agreed by the Six. 'Almost every conceivable Community policy or rule or enactment is the resultant of a conflict of interests between members, and has embedded in it features representing a compromise between these interests,' the chief negotiator, Con O'Neill, complained; 'open it up at any point, and the whole laborious basis of the compromise will fall apart.' So, he concluded, the motto was 'swallow the lot, and swallow it now'.[24]

Prevarication over sovereignty proved hideously expensive. The price was still worth paying, but twenty years of withdrawn recalcitrance had done severe damage to our

economy, our status and our national interests. By the time
Britain acceded, the EEC had already been modelled by a
historic compromise between France and West Germany.
France had assumed the leadership of Europe and achieved
protection for its farmers as well as peace with its neighbour,
thanks to West German acquiescence and funding. In return,
the FRG had won industrial recovery and international
approbation. This bargain was sealed in a budget spent mostly
on the CAP and raised on a formula based on trading levels,
so Britain was hit from both sides. Having thrown away our
strength, we entered from a position of weakness.

### On the fringe

The fact that Wilson immediately reneged on the deal by
reopening negotiations when he returned to power – a
process that inevitably delivered nothing significant – hardly
endeared Britain to the other members. It instantly revealed
the capacity of domestic politics and short-term concerns to
destroy consistent objectives for Britain in Europe. This has
been constantly debilitating, resulting in several missed
chances to seize the initiative and regain a leadership position
on the Continent.

The first came in 1984 when François Mittérrand became
anxious to abandon his three-year experiment with Keyne-
sianism in one country, which had put Socialist France at
odds with Christian Democrat West Germany. After more
than a decade of stagnation he reignited the dynamic
impulses of the Community by laying down an agenda for
agricultural reform, the accession of Portugal and Spain, the
liberalisation of the internal market and an increase in central
funding. Keen to improve relations with Margaret Thatcher,
he also brokered the Fontainebleau Agreement to settle

Britain's claim for a permanent budget rebate system. Improving the CAP, enlargement and free trade were Britain's primary concerns, but Thatcher was so wary of pooled sovereignty and further finance for the Community that she demurred. Mittérrand became sufficiently fed up with her hesitation that to break the logjam he not only turned back to the FRG but also coined the term '*la géométrie variable*' and suggested that Europe should progress at two speeds, allowing France and others to press on while Britain travelled in the slow lane with Denmark.

Our best chance emerged with ideas for a Single Market in 1985. For the first time since before the Schuman Plan, Britain took the lead in Europe, pressing for further pooling of sovereignty to overhaul protectionism and promote competition in the name of our national interests. The momentum soon broke, however, foundering on the rocks of the Social Chapter, the single currency and the reunification of Germany. By opposing all three during 1989, Thatcher effectively excluded Britain from conversations about the future of the continent – languishing in a minority of one – while the dialogue between France and Germany intensified as both became ever more eager to obey Thomas Mann's maxim. They grasped the Delors Report on Economic and Monetary Union, published in April, as a ready-made response to the fall of the Berlin Wall in November, paving the way for two momentous treaties, German Reunification and Maastricht. History marched by Thatcher and Britain.

Although France and Germany, the largest economies in Europe, have forged a close working relationship, it would be a mistake to believe anti-European propaganda that they have simply been grabbing the sovereignty of other members. The others all have determined objectives of their own.

For smaller countries, like the Benelux, the European Union offers access to influence that would otherwise be beyond their reach, and their achievement is reflected in the fact that so many institutions are headquartered in their capitals. Italy looks to Europe for a sense of direction that its national governments have often failed to provide. For the more recent members, the EU underwrites democratic innovations brought about after the fall of dictators in Greece, Portugal and Spain, and it enables economic expansion for Austria, Denmark, Finland, Ireland and Sweden. Although there are challenges to the pro-European consensus in all member states, only the Danes have suffered the divisiveness that has plagued Britain.

When John Major secured opt-outs from the Maastricht provisions for both the Social Chapter and the single currency, a two-speed Europe became a virtual reality. In the beginning he made a virtue of it, arguing that the EU should be 'multi-track, multi-speed, multi-layered', allowing members to proceed at their own pace.[25] Just a few months later, however, he declared that 'I see real danger in talk of a hard core, inner and outer circles, a two-tier Europe. I recoil from ideas of a Union in which some would be more equal than others.'[26] This confusion emerged because Britain had once again chosen to make itself less equal but did not enjoy the consequences. In echoes of Schuman and Messina, Britain flinched from the argument about sovereignty and abdicated influence over Economic and Monetary Union, with little say about the convergence criteria, the structure of the Central Bank or the timetable to introduce the euro. We drifted further from the heart of Europe – preparations for the single currency – and seemed bogged down in trivia that apparently concerned only us.

Clinging to remnants of legal sovereignty rather than deploying effective power, buffeted by events not shaping the direction of the Continent, obsessed by parochial concerns and unable to paint across the European canvas a broader picture of British national interests, there have been innumerable false starts and blind alleys. We have been less at the heart and more an appendix of Europe. It has become a cliché that we have repeatedly missed the European boat, but as history has proved it repeats as farce again and again, surely it is finally time to learn from our mistakes.

## Opportunities and threats

There is no doubt that of the three circles of British influence, Europe has become more central than either the Commonwealth or the United States to our role in the world. Yet our role in Europe remains uncertain. Winston Churchill's argument for pooling sovereignty has been repeated each time we have faced the prospect of further integration, and in the end it has always won out, though not before prevarication has hampered our national interests. The fear in the current debate about the single currency once again threatens to strip our power to press our agenda on other issues, rendering us unable to take advantage of imminent opportunities, notably for enlargement and reform.

### *Enlargement*

Political leaders of all our major parties have consistently championed enlargement to Central and Eastern Europe.[27] The sheer scale of the applications for membership is awesome.[28] In addition to outstanding claims from Turkey,

Cyprus and Malta, ten former communist countries have asked to join: Hungary, Poland, Romania, Slovakia, Latvia, Estonia, Lithuania, Bulgaria, the Czech Republic and Slovenia.[29]

Membership would underpin their political and economic reforms, entrenching liberal democracy, just as it did in Greece, Portugal and Spain. If the petitions are rejected, or if the accession negotiations are dragged out, then progress may be stalled and aggressive nationalism might return. Furthermore, it would send a terrible signal to other potential applicants, especially those from the Balkans. If the overtures are accepted, however, there would be great benefits to Britain. Potential hazards on our furthest borders – including security dangers, environmental pollution and organised crime – would be addressed. Most important, the internal market would grow from 370 million to 500 million consumers, offering new trade routes that we are well placed to exploit because we already export more than £3 billion a year to the twelve countries currently in negotiations.

Yet integrating such a politically and economically diverse group challenges the old order and offers some existing members a reason to procrastinate. The Irish are particularly concerned that they will lose out on subsidies if these relatively poor countries join. In fact, the whole process has already been held up for far too long. Without a platform from which Britain can press for enlargement, it might be further delayed or even derailed.

## Political reform

British governments of every hue have long stressed the need to improve Europe's institutions, to expedite enlargement, address the perceived absence of democratic legitimacy and entrench the control of the members. But our views have rarely received the hearing our status deserves, thanks to our frequent belligerence and worries about sovereignty.

However, debate in Europe about the future of the Union has recently taken a new turn. It has been helped by academics like Larry Siedentop, whose influential book *Democracy in Europe* called for a constitutional settlement to define and limit the role of Brussels.[30] It will come to a head at the Inter-Governmental Conference scheduled for 2004, where members will battle for their national interests and establish a framework for the following decade.

Ahead of the IGC leaders from across the Continent have already started outlining their ambitions.[31] Although every utterance by any European leader is exaggerated by anti-Europeans and held up as proof of a concerted drive for a 'superstate', there is now a significant divergence of opinion between France and Germany, and for that matter a lack of consensus within either country. This is a far cry from the dominant days of Valéry Giscard d'Estaing and Helmut Schmidt in the 1970s and François Mittérrand and Helmut Kohl in the 1980s.

When Jacques Chirac, the Gaullist French President, called for a 'pioneer group' of countries to forge ahead without the others, anti-Europeans were up in arms; but the idea garnered little support and has since been quietly dropped. In any case it was outflanked by talk of 'enhanced cooperation' in various fields by differing groups of countries – a flexible approach more to the taste of the British government – which was originally raised by Lionel Jospin, the Socialist French Prime Minister who hopes to replace Chirac as President. Jospin later proposed 'economic government of the euro-zone', a suggestion overhyped by anti-Europeans here but one that received a very cool response across the Continent, not least in Berlin.

Meanwhile, Gerhard Schröder, the Socialist German Chancellor, floated thoughts that were summarised by the headline writers as a demand for 'European government'; although less well reported, he also argued for a clearer delineation of authority between Brussels and the nations, precautions against the creeping transfer of competencies to the centre and even the repatriation of some powers back to the members. Not only did Paris disown stronger European government, so did Joschka Fischer, the Green German Foreign Minister.

This lack of a coherent Franco-German narrative presents a historic opportunity for Britain to help lead the debate by acting as a chief power broker. Our consensus is instinctively closer to France on the political issues (for the supremacy of the nation) but nearer to Germany on the economic questions (for limited central funding); but we can also build bridges on behalf of those countries that feel they have had insufficient influence in previous negotiations. There will no doubt be profound disagreements about matters of detail but the tide is flowing in the direction we would choose, so we can guide the ship more successfully than before provided we are seen to be committed to the journey.

To allay fears that Brussels is gathering power at the expense of members, Britain has called for a new Statement of Principles to define those areas of supranational competence and those that are rightfully the responsibility of nations. Article 3b of the Maastricht Treaty provided that 'the Community shall take action, in accordance with the principle of subsidiarity, only if and in so far as the objectives of the proposed action cannot be sufficiently achieved by Member

States' and can 'be better achieved by the Community'. There is now growing pressure to concretise this notion, putting formal limits to the pooling of sovereignty, by emphasising that only certain decisions should be properly integrated while others need admit little or no joint control.

While it is true that European institutions suffer an apparent 'democratic deficit', the national model based solely on direct elections cannot be transposed to a Union of states precisely because it is not itself a state. Its members are countries, so representations have to come not just from citizens, as in the European Parliament, but from governments, as in the Council of Ministers and the European Council of heads of government. To strengthen the role of governments, Britain has proposed that the European Council should publish an annual work programme and meet more often than once every three months to monitor the output of the European Commission, which is after all akin to its civil service. And to better involve other national politicians, Britain has suggested that national parliaments should send delegates to sit in a new second chamber responsible for monitoring the application of the subsidiarity principle.

The prospect of enlargement requires the EU to be flexible enough to cater for twenty-five or more members, which has opened debate about further changes to institutions that were originally designed by and for the first Six.[32] The Commission is particularly vulnerable to criticism, not least because of the uncovering of a corruption scandal in 1999. That crisis undermined its authority and has now sparked a process of root and branch reform that is genuinely attacking vested interests. The Commission is not the untamed monster of anti-European mythology however. Its staff totals 17,000, including 11,000 translators and secretaries, leaving

only 6,000 administrators, the demonised 'Brussels bureaucrats'; by comparison Birmingham City Council has a staff of
52,000. And although it has the right to initiate activity in
some areas, about 35 per cent of its proposals implement
international agreements, 30 per cent modernise old rules, 20
per cent follow a request from the Council or Parliament and
10 per cent are routine matters like the annual fixing of farm
prices, so just 5 per cent come from under its own steam. But
it must be seen to earn its right to govern.

The Parliament, the only internationally elected such
body in the world, also needs to burnish its reputation for
competence and probity following concern at its gravy train
image. It has provided a positive check on the Commission –
usefully amending proposals and forcing the resignation of
Commissioners after the corruption scandal broke – but to
win more responsibility it must be seen to behave more
responsibly.

The Court of Justice is the ultimate legal arbiter of the
EU.[33] As such, its very existence is frequently attacked by
anti-Europeans who aim to discredit the Union; but without
enforcement of the rules, the whole thing would fall apart
and even the internal market could not operate. The Court
works well but could work better, acting fairly, firmly and
fast. Fairly, to enforce the subsidiarity principle by ferociously
guarding national competences from encroachment by the
Commission, as it did when it ruled in 1988 that the decision
to permit Sunday trading was a matter for Britain not
Europe. Firmly, to ensure all members enact all rules, though
it is simply not true that Britain alone comprehensively
implements EU legislation.[34] And fast, to overturn injustices,
a requirement highlighted by the plodding process of bringing France to book for illegally banning British beef.

Britain could offer particular lessons to the Central Bank, whose management has been criticised as feeble. It has especially been accused of having too much independence and too little accountability. It could benefit from following the Bank of England model where officials have freedom of operation – to set interest rates – but the objective – the inflation target – is laid down by political masters. It might also make its inflation target symmetrical and copy the practice of publishing its minutes. But our ability to lead the argument for reform will be minimal if we stay outside the euro-zone.

Of course it is unlikely that Britain will win on all these items, but they are all on the agenda. In the past our interventions have too often been limited to simply shouting about sovereignty, and at the very least we now have an opportunity to make a telling contribution that would benefit ourselves. We must not squander it.

### Economic reform

Events are blowing the winds of change not only through the EU institutions but across the European economies too, and economics has been one of the priorities of successive British governments. During the long years in the wilderness between 1950 and 1973, cut off from the rapidly expanding markets on the Continent and protected from competitive pressures, our relative decline put us in no position to lecture others; but in the 1980s and 1990s we caught up with the major Continental countries in many areas.[35] While we still have lessons to learn and desperately need increased investment in skills and infrastructure, we finally have sufficient credibility to help lead the economic argument.[36]

The problem should not be overstated. Anti-Europeans are wrong to raise scares about a supposedly sclerotic social model that they claim is suffocating the EU and threatening to seep across the Channel. European inefficiencies are no danger to British prosperity; it is more that greater Continental competitiveness would present us with even better opportunities to expand into foreign markets. In any case, most of the EU is richer than we are because on GDP per head we come only tenth in the league table.[37] And most of the EU is more efficient than we are because on productivity per worker we come only twelfth in the league table, well below the average.[38]

The Single Market was a powerful motor for structural corrections, although there needs to be further liberalisation to promote competition, notably in aviation, energy, financial services, telecoms and utilities. The single currency has been driving reforms even faster. The Maastricht criteria galvanised the political will to push forward difficult measures, instilling fiscal and monetary discipline, that are now reaping rewards across the euro-zone as public debt has shrunk, inflation has been brought under control and interest rates have been held down.

Before the advent of the euro, it was easy for national policies to footle around on the demand side, particularly tinkering with interest rates. Now that they are set elsewhere, deeper problems on the supply side cannot be ignored and attention has shifted to reforming fundamentals to raise the long-term employment potential. *Dirigisme* is out and market dynamism is in because national economies must be flexible enough to adjust smoothly to local shocks. And as the single currency allows companies to expand and operate with the same economies of scale that previously advantaged US firms, national governments are forced to create an environment that attracts enterprise.

In some areas Britain has led by example because other countries have seen how a commitment to supply-side reform has improved our appeal to business, not least inward investors. Moreover, Britain has constructed a consensus for common action. The Lisbon summit in 2000 agreed 'a new strategic goal' of making the EU 'the most competitive and dynamic knowledge-based economy in the world' within ten years, reaching real annual growth rates of 3 per cent and creating 20 million net new jobs.[39] The reforms under way are rarely suited to screaming headlines, and there will no doubt be setbacks and uneven progress, but taken together they represent a profound shift in policy, notably cutting taxation, that is already starting to pay dividends, especially in reducing unemployment.

Taxes are falling, by about 1.5 points a year. Europe has a relatively high tax burden – 44 per cent of GDP compared to 30 per cent in the US and 28 per cent in Japan – skewed towards social security contributions. But as jobs are generated, tax and benefit systems take less strain. This has allowed Germany to plan an aggressive programme that has forced corporation tax down from 52 per cent to 39 per cent and over the next four years it is to push the basic rate of income tax down from 23 per cent to 15 per cent and the top rate from 51 per cent to 42 per cent. France is cutting taxes on small and medium-sized enterprises, and Greece, Ireland, Portugal and Spain all now have lower taxes than Britain.

Most important, unemployment is falling too. There have been particular problems in Germany since reunification, as well as in France and Spain, and if all members were to match the best rates in the EU then an additional 30 million people would be in work. But during 2000 the impact of reform pushed unemployment below 10 per cent for the first time in Germany since 1995 and in France since 1991, while Spanish unemployment has plummeted by more than a third in the past three years.

The pressure for economic and political reform, spurred by the prospect of enlargement, has opened a golden opportunity for Britain to forge the kind of Europe that would suit us better. Margaret Thatcher's government was isolated by choice and John Major's was hindered by division, but Tony Blair's has been given a chance to lead. Events have set in train a process that looks for its ideas from beyond the traditional sources of France and Germany, and the debate is now about the speed not the direction of reform. To lead, we need to see cooperation not as a threat to our independence but as an opportunity to increase our power.

## The choice: isolated or engaged

Anti-Europeans conclude from Britain's failure to always get our own way on the Continent that we will forever fall victim to a hostile foreign majority. Hence they are determined that we should abandon attempts to work with our partners and withdraw into splendid isolation. But the lesson of history is surely that despite our inability to resolve our dilemma over sovereignty and thus fashion a leadership role, we have still won huge benefits from Europe and with a more enlightened approach we could achieve even more now. As the European Union leaps forward again – enlarged by its biggest influx of members and committed to radical reform – Britain has another, perhaps in our era final, genuine chance to maximise our leverage over events that affect us deeply.

The real choice facing the nation is not between those who claim to defend British, or rather English, exceptionalism from European interference and those who would pawn our independence to a phantom 'superstate'. It is between those who have sufficient confidence in our country to advance our national interests through meaningful engagement in Europe and those who would have us retreat further into an insular nationalism that has already held us back for fifty years. In this decision the single currency is the fork in the road.

### Norway with nuclear weapons

Currently the most fashionable preference among those wary of Europe is for what might be termed the 'Danish model' – in the EU but out of the euro. Although it may seem bizarre to be guided by the aspirations of just 5 million people living in an economy with limited exposure to currency fluctuations, this is the backstop for many reasonable people and the opening gambit of anti-Europeans who wish to embark on the road to complete withdrawal.[40]

Even taken at face value as an honest ambition, defenders of what they believe to be the current state of affairs are wrong to imagine that a decision not to join would return Britain to the status quo ante. Many would doubtless prefer that the euro had never been invented, and some have openly wished it would collapse and disappear, but it is a reality. The debate, which has long been about the rights and wrongs of a single currency in principle, must now consider whether we enter or ignore a project that is going ahead anyway. It is not possible to revert to the world as it was before 1 January 1999 and we cannot avoid the consequences of turning our back on a system already used by 300 million people on our doorstep.

If we ignore the single currency it is overwhelmingly likely there would be a drop in exports, a flight of inward investment and a loss of jobs. There would also be a significant opportunity cost. British businesses would be hampered by unique competitive disadvantages, our shoppers would miss out on lower prices and our homeowners would not be able to access cheaper mortgages. We would suffer the increasing volatility of sterling with its attendant transaction costs and exchange rate risks. There may be no sudden calamity, but in ten or fifteen years we would wake up and wonder why we had fallen behind. After all, that is exactly what happened when we rejected the EEC.

There would be perilous political repercussions too. We would have sent a strong signal to our partners about our lack of commitment to the EU, and a half-in half-out half-hearted membership with no seat at the tables where important economic decisions are taken, such as the European Central Bank and the euro-group, would at the very least entrench a two-tier Europe with Britain trapped in subservience. This is the modern incarnation of the age-old fear that the countries of Europe would band together at best without, at worst against, us. Avoiding this spectre has been the dominant theme of British foreign policy for centuries, from attempts to maintain the balance of power through to efforts by Margaret Thatcher and John Major to thwart the emergence of a core group of members in the EU, and we would have brought it upon ourselves once again.

Some people no doubt innocently believe that Britain could reject the single currency without affecting our place in Europe, but it is a wolf in sheep's clothing. For others, disrupting Britain's relations with the EU is the principal reason for opposing the euro. They are trying to spark an acrimonious row that could only be resolved by Britain withdrawing and blaming foreigners for our isolation. That is the logic, and the stated ambition, of this position.

Anti-Europeans trumpet a bewildering cacophony of isolationist options. The starkest is simple solitude, ambitiously known as the 'Greenland model'. Greenland – with a population of just 50,000 living more than 1,000 miles from mainland Europe – is the only territory to have left the European institutional framework. Although still a Danish possession, Greenland was granted home rule in 1979 and in 1982 voted in a referendum for symbolic freedom from Denmark by leaving the EEC. Greenland is now counted as an 'overseas country and territory' of the EU, just like some former British, French and Dutch colonies.

Even most anti-Europeans rarely advocate Greenland as the lodestar for a successful industrial and trading nation. So to make separation seem more palatable, they suggest we should throw in our lot with the United States by joining the North American Free Trade Agreement or use the European Economic Area to negotiate access to the internal market while avoiding the political implications of the EU.

Britain exports 57 per cent of our goods to our near neighbours in the EU, and just 16 per cent to our distant cousins in the US and 2 per cent to Canada and Mexico. Less than 5 per cent of US trade is with Britain, most of which is already tariff-free. As Britain conducts almost four times as much trade with the EU as with NAFTA, it would put ideological dogma over economic sanity to leave one for the other. It would reduce our clout in the world too. The former Conservative Cabinet Minister William Waldegrave, a fan of this 'Canadian model', accepts it would mean 'no sitting at the top table anymore' and 'no more punching above our weight'. And he acknowledges that 'after a decade or two, we would have as little say over what happened in our end of the continent as do the Canadians in theirs: not *no* say, but not much say'.[41]

Anti-Europeans also urge the 'Norwegian model', of enrolment in the EEA, their beloved free trade area. Along with Iceland and Liechtenstein – the other non-EU members of the EEA – Norway enjoys access to the internal market. However, in return it also implements the entire apparatus of EU law, enforced by the European Court of Justice, while having no say whatsoever in its formulation. This is the arid sovereignty that the anti-European alternative boils down to: Britain should aspire to become like Norway with nuclear weapons.

To settle in an outer tier of part-time membership, semi-detached and quarantined from the important decisions that affect us. Or to withdraw altogether, totally divorced from the developing European superpower twenty miles from our shores. Those are the options. Either way, our economy would suffer, exposed to the chill winds of globalisation. Either way, we would be left unable to shape the EU as it grows ever more influential over our own destiny, in or out. And either way, it would stunt our national identity by turning us inward to an insecure nationalism. Running away from the argument is a modern policy of appeasement: it is our duty to stand and fight for Britain.

Neither marginalisation nor disengagement could possibly resolve the confusion about Britishness. Europe will not go away. It would continue to flourish without us just as it did following our failure to join the Schuman Plan and the Messina Conference. The debate about our economic stability and our role in the world would continue to turn on

developments in Europe just as it did from 1950 to 1973.
Like it or not, Britain cannot resist the magnetic pull of
Europe. After all, we declined a say in 1950–2 and again in
1955–7 but still applied to join later on; we were twice
knocked back but became so desperate to get in that we took
whatever terms were on offer the third time around. Outside
the EU or just outside the euro the agony of our national
introspection about what it means to be British would be
prolonged while we retreated into the shell of our former
glory. We would probably join in the end anyway, when it
was too late to do anything but embrace an enterprise that
had already been determined by others who had no reason
to take account of our interests. But there is another way.

### The great patriotic cause of our age

The purpose of any government must be to maximise the
security and prosperity of its people. Every prime minister
since Harold Macmillan through Margaret Thatcher to Tony
Blair has realised that these ends are better served in Europe
than in isolation. With varying degrees of enthusiasm, they
have all persuaded a reluctant public to accept it too. But
lately the mood has been darkening. The complexities of
dealing with a rapidly changing Europe combined with a
full-blooded anti-European campaign have opened a mismatch between the self-confessed ignorance and apparent
scepticism of public opinion and what is actually best for our
country. Emotion is again overshadowing reason, driven by
myths and fears. To break out of this box there is urgent need
for the pro-Britain, pro-Europe argument to be made and
heard.

An extraordinary notion has long been propagated by
some opponents of Britain's place in Europe, and gone vir-

tually unchecked in the quarter-century since the referendum that overwhelmingly confirmed our membership; it has now contaminated the debate about whether or not we should join the single currency. It is the idea that to be pro-European is to be anti-British and that the best way to stand up for Britain is to retreat behind our moat and be at best wary of, at worst hostile to, working too closely with our ancient Continental rivals. But this is the false prophecy of bogus patriots.

The debate about Europe in Britain needs to revolve around an entirely different axis to that dictated by anti Europeans in recent years. The pro-Europe argument is not anti-British. It is exactly the opposite. It stems from the patriotic appetite to see our country thrive at the start of the new century, not stand aside from vital European developments that affect us, as we did in the second half of the old. The pro-Britain, pro-Europe case comes from the desire to regain our confidence and fulfil our potential. Only by allowing our reason to overcome our prejudice can we escape from the romantic fantasies that paralyse our national ambitions: instead of simply shouting 'Britain is best' we need a rational assessment of what is best for Britain.

Most of the opposition to Europe and the euro is driven not by economics but by politics. Lurking behind the dogma is a mistaken Little England view of history in which Britain does best when detached and isolated, while engaging in Europe is portrayed as a betrayal of what it means to be British. In truth Britain is changing, struggling to come to terms with the confusing realities that have crept up on us since the end of the Second World War and the collapse of the Empire, and a vociferous minority has been preying on the insecurity this has induced, inventing the threat of a 'superstate' as a modern 'hostile Other' to undermine our role in Europe.

But Britain is stronger within Europe, where Britishness is perfectly secure. During the 1975 referendum nobody understood this more clearly than Margaret Thatcher. 'It is a myth that our membership of the Community will suffocate national tradition and culture. Are the Germans any less German for being in the Community, or the French any less French? Of course they are not! It seems to me to display an amazing lack of self-confidence in Britain on the part of some people, that they think that, whereas no other nation in the Community has lost its national character, Britain in some way will,' she said.[42]

That very same argument needs to hold sway again today, overcoming the fears of Europe that have held us back for half a century. Divisions within political parties and indecision by governments of all parties have rendered British policy towards Europe inconsistent and confused for far too long. The political consequence has been a decline in the popularity of Europe in Britain, tempting us to make the wrong decisions for our country. The economic cost has been recurrent instability and relative decline, while the diplomatic price has been a loss of international influence. To break with this legacy, and overturn the growing scepticism that is preventing us from taking an informed decision about whether or not to join the euro, the prime task of explaining the importance of Europe to Britain must rest with our political leaders. As Tony Blair put it at the launch of 'Britain in Europe', 'Once in each generation, the case for Britain in Europe needs to be remade, from first principles. The time for this generation is now.'[43] It is now time to honour that promise, to end the decades of dithering and finally provide honest leadership.

While Britain simply cannot afford to go it alone, with all the risk that would entail, the benefits of the European Union and the potential advantages of the single currency are manifold. We have the chance to boost our prosperity, improve the quality of our lives and use our unique platform as a gateway to Europe and a bridge to the world to enhance our global standing. When Britain plays a leading part, as with the construction of the Single Market, Europe works better. For its own sake as well as ours, Europe must ring with a British accent. Although we have to become more understanding of European differences, to invert Thomas Mann's motto we need to see a more British Europe not just a more European Britain.

We have a chance to seize the initiative. The high tide of the Franco-German partnership has receded as Europe increasingly looks to other experiences to lead political and economic reform to accompany enlargement to the former Soviet satellites. Far from driving to a 'superstate', a new pluralism beckons. Of course Franco-German relations will continue to be vital to Europe, but there is space to recast the *entente cordiale* with room for a triangular or multilateral relationship involving Britain. But little can be achieved from an outer tier.

The decision on the euro is probably the most important we will face in our generation, but it often seems that the years of argument have generated such heat that it will prevent much light from ever breaking through. In fact, the balance of economic evidence augurs for joining as soon as the conditions allow. If we do not enter in this parliament we may have missed our chance for a decade. The next election will not be until 2005 or 2006 and any government elected then may have less confidence than the one recently

returned with a landslide majority of 167; even if it held and
won a referendum within its first couple of years, it would
then need to negotiate the terms of entry so Britain could
not actually join until around 2010. That would feel like the
kind of delay that damaged us so badly when we hesitated
over the EEC.

Britons will not vote for the single currency until they are
convinced of the economic benefits for themselves and their
country. But even that may not be enough. Healing the running sore of argument about our relations with Europe will
also require resolving the apparent identity crisis that has
begun to afflict us.

The real question we must answer is not 'What does it
mean to be British these days?' but 'What kind of country do
we want to become?' Of course we must not jettison our history, but neither must we be held prisoners by our past.
Anti-Europeans are wrong to blame Europe for our national
insecurity. European centralists are equally wrong to claim
that Britain is an artificial creation whose bonds are loosen-
ing thanks partly to the appeal of European citizenship.
Britain is alive and well, but ours is a different country in a
different world to that of our parents and grandparents.

In the past half-century Britain has changed. Britain's
place in the world has been transformed too. The props of
Commonwealth preferences and a special relationship with
the United States are no longer strong enough to support the
global reach we previously enjoyed. We must come to terms
with the fact that while Britain is still a great nation it is no
longer the Great Power it was in 1945. In any case in the turbulent modern world interconnected threats challenge all
countries to pool their sovereignty to create international
and supranational responses. The simple truth is that the

European Union is a useful vehicle for any British government to protect the security and prosperity of our people in
the age of globalisation.

Britain faces a historic decision. But it is not the false
choice that is suffocating the current debate, between standing up for Britain against Europe and dissolving our national
identity in an imaginary 'superstate'. The real choice is
between pretending we can return Britain to our glorious
but fading past and confronting the reality of striving to
advance our national interests through meaningful engagement in Europe. The outcome, which will determine our
future for years ahead, rests on the single currency. To make
the best choice for Britain we need to build a healthy consensus, based on a patriotism of national purpose that puts a
proper understanding of our national interests before visceral
fears of Europe. That is why pro-Europeanism is truly the
great patriotic cause of our age.

# Acknowledgements

This book is primarily about Britain, and how our relationship with the other countries of the European Union impacts upon us. Although there is a vast library on this topic from those who are wary of or hostile to our involvement in Europe, and there are many political memoirs and academic tomes that cover parts of the story in detail, the literature for the general reader from pro-Europeans is tiny. I am therefore more indebted than most authors to the advice of my many friends who have offered support during this project.

For commenting on early drafts I am particularly grateful to Paul Adamson, Graham Bishop, Terry Bishop, Leslie Butterfield, Christopher Johnson, Roger Liddle, John Pinder, Chris Powell, Giles and Lisanne Radice, Neil Sherlock, Guy Walker, Ernest Wistrich and several others who wished to remain nameless.

Board and Council members and other senior figures at 'Britain in Europe' have proved a constant source of learning and guidance, and special tribute is due to our staff, who frequently give way beyond the call of duty: Anna A, Anna C, Anna Y, Ann, Barbara, Caroline, Ceri, Chris, Claire, Danny, David, Diane, Estelle, Fiona, Gary, George, Hannah, Jessica, Jim, Justin, Katrina, Keith, Lucy, Nick, Paul, Richard,

Stephen, Steve, Tony, Vikki and Wesley.

For their love and encouragement, despite my long periods of solitude in the office, I owe Gloria, Tim, Kevin and Jackie. And of course I would like to thank Andrew Franklin and his team at Profile for editing and publishing my work.

# Notes

## Chapter 1

1 In addition to the sources cited below, see especially
Jonathan Freedland – *Bring Home the Revolution: The
Case for a British Republic* (Fourth Estate, London, 1998),
Norman Davies – *The Isles: A History* (Macmillan,
London, 1999), Bhikhu Parekh (ed) – *The Future of
Multi-Ethnic Britain* (Profile, London, 2000), Jeremy
Paxman – *The English: A Portrait of a People* (Michael
Joseph, London, 1998), Peter Hitchens – *The Abolition of
Britain: From Lady Chatterley to Tony Blair* (Quartet,
London, 1999) and Andrew Marr – *The Day Britain
Died* (Profile, London, 2000).

2 John Major – speech to Conservative Group for
Europe, 22 April 1993.

3 John Townend – speech to East Yorkshire Conservative
Association, 21 March 2001.

4 John Townend – letter to Gurbux Singh, chair of the
Commission for Racial Equality, 26 April 2001.

5 William Hague – speech to Conservative Party Spring
Forum, 4 March 2001.

6 These arguments are worked through in Benedict

Anderson – *Imagined Communities: Reflections on the Origin and Spread of Nationalism* (Verso, London, 1983) and Eric Hobsbawm & Terence Ranger (eds) – *The Invention of Tradition* (CUP, Cambridge, 1983).

7   Linda Colley – *Britons: Forging the Nation, 1707–1837* (Yale, London, 1992), p. 5.

8   *Ibid* p. 7.

9   Tom Nairn – *The Break-up of Britain* (New Left Books, London, 1977) and Tom Nairn – *After Britain* (Granta, London, 2000).

10  Simon Heffer – *Nor Shall My Sword: The Reinvention of England* (Weidenfeld & Nicolson, London, 1999), p. 133.

11  Stephen Haseler – *The English Tribe: Identity, Nation and Europe* (Macmillan, London, 1996), p. ix.

12  *Ibid* pp. 3–4.

13  *Ibid* p. 152.

14  *British and European Social Attitudes: 15th Report, 1998–99* (Ashgate, Aldershot, 1998), pp. 1–16.

15  A collection of essays by leading Britons acclaiming various icons of Britishness is published in John Mitchinson (ed) – *British Greats* (Cassell, London, 2000).

16  Yasmin Alibhai-Brown – *Who Do We Think We Are? Imagining the New Britain* (Allen Lane, London, 2000), p. 271.

17  Richard Crossman – *The Diaries of a Cabinet Minister, vol II* (Hamish Hamilton, London, 1976), p. 83.

18  Michael Foot – speech to Labour Party Conference, 4 October 1973.

19  Peter Shore – speech to Labour Party Conference, 4 October 1973.

20  Tony Benn – *Arguments For Socialism* (Jonathan Cape, London, 1979), p. 95.

21   Stanley Baldwin – speech to Royal Society of St
      George, 6 May 1924.

22   *Daily Telegraph*, 18 July 1997.

23   *This England*, Summer 1997.

24   Linda Proud & Valerie Petts – *Consider England*
      (Shepheard-Walwyn, London, 1994), Peter Vansittart –
      *In Memory of England: A Novelist's View of History* (John
      Murray, London, 1998), Roger Scruton – *England: An
      Elegy* (Chatto & Windus, London, 2000) and Richard
      Body – *England for the English* (New European
      Publications, London, 2001).

25   Clive Aslet – *Anyone for England? A Search for British
      Identity* (Little Brown, London, 1997), p. 22.

26   Ian Buruma – *Voltaire's Coconuts: or Anglomania in Europe*
      (Weidenfeld & Nicolson, London, 1999), pp. 283–96.

27   David Willets – speech to Centre for Policy Studies, 8
      October 1998.

28   Julian Barnes – *England, England* (Jonathan Cape,
      London, 1998).

29   John Arbuthnot – *The History of John Bull* (OUP,
      Oxford, 1976), p. 9.

30   Michael Portillo – speech to Conservative Party
      Conference, 10 October 1995.

31   Peter Tapsell – speech to Louth and Horncastle
      Conservative Association, 11 May 2001.

32   Andrew Roberts – *The Aachen Memorandum* (Orion,
      London, 1996).

33   John Redwood – *The Death of Britain? The UK's
      Constitutional Crisis* (Macmillan, London, 1999), p. 8.

34   Alan Macfarlane – *The Origins of English Individualism:
      The Family, Property and Social Transition* (Basil Blackwell,
      Oxford, 1978), p. 163.

35  William Hague – speech to Centre for Policy Studies,
    24 January 1999.
36  William Hague – speech to Conservative Party
    Conference, 7 October 1999.
37  George Orwell – *The Lion and the Unicorn: Socialism and
    the English Genius* (Penguin, London, 1982), p. 35.
38  *Life*, 9 May 1969.
39  Bill Bryson – *Notes From A Small Island* (Doubleday,
    London, 1995), p. 32.
40  W. C. Sellar & R. J. Yeatman – *1066 And All That*
    (Methuen, London, 1999), p. 25.
41  *Ibid* p. 123.
42  *Sun*, 4 June 1975.

## Chapter 2

1   Dean Acheson – speech to West Point Military
    Academy, 6 December 1962.
2   *Ibid*.
3   Quoted in Hugo Young – *This Blessed Plot: Britain and
    Europe from Churchill to Blair* (Macmillan, London,
    1998), p. 24.
4   This thesis is outlined in the title and content of the
    seminal Michael Charlton – *The Price of Victory* (BBC,
    London, 1983).
5   Jean Monnet – *Memoirs* (Collins, London, 1978), p. 293.
6   *Ibid* p. 308.
7   H. Young, pp. 54–5.
8   H. Young, p. 56.
9   Quoted in John W. Young – *Britain and European Unity,
    1945–99* (Macmillan, London, 2000), p. 41.

10  H. Young, p. 89.
11  Paul-Henri Spaak – *The Continuing Battle: Memoirs of a European 1936–1966* (Weidenfeld & Nicolson, London, 1971), p. 232.
12  H. Young, p. 91.
13  H. Young, p. 93.
14  Harold Macmillan – *Britain, the Commonwealth and Europe* (Conservative Political Centre, London, 1962).
15  H. Young, p. 190.
16  The United Kingdom and the European Communities (Cmnd 4715, HMSO White Paper, July 1971).
17  *Ibid.*
18  Edward Heath, Hansard col 2202–12, 28 October 1971.
19  'Why you should vote No', statement by the National Referendum Campaign, May 1975.
20  'Why you should vote Yes', statement by 'Britain in Europe', May 1975.
21  Margaret Thatcher, Hansard col 1021–33, 8 April 1975.
22  David Butler & Uwe Kitzinger – *The 1975 Referendum* (Macmillan, London, 1976), p. 273.
23  Michael Heseltine – 'Britain's Place in Europe', in David Curry et al – *The Conservative Tradition in Europe* (Conservative Mainstream, London, 1998), p. 19.
24  H. Young, p. 332.
25  H. Young, p. 310.
26  *Spectator*, 14 July 1990.
27  *Independent on Sunday*, 15 July 1990.
28  Douglas Hurd – speech to Scottish Conservative Party Conference, 11 May 1990.
29  Margaret Thatcher, Hansard col 869–90, 30 October 1990.
30  Geoffrey Howe, Hansard col 461–5, 13 November 1990.

31  John Major – speech to Konrad Adenauer Foundation, 11 March 1991.

32  Quoted in Giles Radice – *Offshore: Britain and the European Idea* (I. B. Tauris, London, 1992), p. 88.

33  John Major – *The Autobiography* (HarperCollins, London, 1999), pp. 343–4.

34  William Cash – *Against A Federal Europe: The Battle for Britain* (Duckworth, London, 1991), pp. 41, 82.

35  Michael Spicer – *A Treaty Too Far: A New Policy for Europe* (Fourth Estate, London, 1992).

36  Norman Lamont – speech to Selsdon Group, 11 October 1994.

37  *Sun*, 4 March 1998 (bananas, cucumbers and apples), *Daily Mail*, 10 August 1995 (mushy peas), *Times*, 27 January 1999 (shandy), *Times*, 15 June 1998 (smacking), *Sunday Telegraph*, 3 October 1993 (whelks), *Daily Telegraph*, 3 December 1994 (summer holidays), *Daily Mail*, 5 April 1994 (MOT), *Sunday Telegraph*, 29 March 1998 (clotted cream), *European*, 6 April 1998 (brandy butter), *Daily Mail*, 19 May 1999 (nuts), *Sunday Times*, 9 April 1995 (toilets) and *Mail on Sunday*, 5 February 1995 (voltage).

38  The most relentlessly haunted by imaginary ghosts in Brussels is Christopher Booker. His stories appear every week in *The Sunday Telegraph* and many of his early tales are collected in Christopher Booker & Richard North – *The Mad Officials: How the Bureaucrats are Strangling Britain* (Constable, London, 1994) and Christopher Booker & Richard North – *The Castle of Lies: Why Britain Must Get Out of Europe* (Duckworth, London, 1996).

39  *Sun*, 6 June 2000.

40  *Sun*, 24 October 2000.
41  Peter J. Anderson & Anthony Weymouth – *Insulting the Public? The British Press and the European Union* (Longman, London, 1999), pp. 184–5.
42  *Daily Telegraph*, 15 October 1998.
43  *Sun*, 24 June 1998.
44  *Daily Telegraph*, 18 May 2001.
45  *Guardian*, 22 January 2001.
46  *Britain*, Anti-Common Market League quarterly bulletin, Autumn 1998.
47  CAFE website (www.cafe.org.uk), 4 August 1999.
48  Rodney Leach – speech to European Foundation, 13 May 1994.
49  Bruges Group website (www.brugesgroup.com), 8 June 2001.
50  *Times*, 21 August 1999.
51  *BBC Breakfast with Frost*, 10 October 1999.
52  *European Journal*, May 1997.
53  *Times*, 14 August 1999.
54  Michael Portillo – speech to Centre for Policy Studies, 21 October 1999.
55  Iain Duncan Smith – speech to Westminster Conservative Association, 3 July 2001.
56  Margaret Thatcher – speech to Conservative Party rally in Plymouth, 22 May 2001.
57  *BBC Today*, 23 May 2001.
58  *Daily Telegraph*, 12 September 2000.
59  *Sunday Telegraph*, 16 June 1996.
60  *Times*, 5 October 1999.
61  BBC news, 5 October 1999.
62  *Daily Telegraph*, 19 June 1996.

## Chapter 3

1   *BBC Today*/ICM, 31 January 2000. The poll, a wake-up
    call for pro-Europeans, showed that 34 per cent
    favoured withdrawal and 53 per cent supported
    membership.

2   Eurobarometer, April 2001. As a rule, those who believe
    themselves to be well informed also tend to be the most
    pro-European: across the EU as a whole, among those
    who describe themselves as well informed about the
    single currency 66 per cent are in favour and just 29 per
    cent are against, but among those who say they are not
    only 45 per cent are in favour with 44 per cent against.

3   Organisation for Economic Co-operation and
    Development.

4   Office of National Statistics.

5   During 2000 the top ten export markets for British
    goods were the United States, Germany, France, the
    Netherlands, Ireland, Belgium–Luxembourg, Italy,
    Spain, Sweden and Japan; and the top ten suppliers of
    goods to Britain were Germany, the United States,
    France, the Netherlands, Belgium–Luxembourg, Italy,
    Japan, Ireland, Spain and Hong Kong.

6   The share of goods exported to the EU was revealed in
    HM Customs and Excise – *UK Regional Trade Estimates*
    (April 2001). The number of jobs dependent on this
    trade was identified in South Bank University European
    Institute – *UK Jobs Dependent on the EU* (February
    2000). The breakdown is:

| Region/Nation | Share of goods exported to the EU | Number of jobs dependent |
|---|---|---|
| Yorkshire & Humberside | 63% | 314,687 |
| North East | 76% | 141,561 |
| North West | 63% | 404,881 |
| East of England | 54% | 300,164 |
| East Midlands | 51% | 291,613 |
| West Midlands | 58% | 381,671 |
| London | 43% | 387,826 |
| South East | 56% | 426,394 |
| South West | 71% | 267,385 |
| England | 56% | 2,916,182 |
| Northern Ireland | 59% | 87,593 |
| Scotland | 69% | 286,628 |
| Wales | 71% | 155,246 |

7   European Commission – *The Impact and Effectiveness of the Single Market* (EC, Brussels, 1996).

8   The Lomé Convention of 1975, updated by the Cotonou Convention of 2000, is a comprehensive trade and aid agreement between the EU and 71 developing countries in Africa, the Caribbean and the Pacific, including many Commonwealth nations. It allows them free access to the internal market for most industrial and agricultural products.

9   Margaret Thatcher – *The Path to Power* (HarperCollins, London, 1995), pp. 126–7.

10  The United Nations Conference on Trade and Development – *World Investment Report 2000*.

11  In 2000 'Britain in Europe' commissioned three separate studies to establish the level of British job dependence on trade with the EU. The overall conclusions were these: Cambridge Econometrics – *UK Job Dependence on*

*Exports to the EU* (February 2000) estimated 2,500,000 jobs; National Institute of Economic and Social Research (NIESR) – *Continent Cut Off? The Macroeconomic Impact of British Withdrawal from the EU* (February 2000) estimated 3,200,000 jobs; and South Bank University European Institute – *UK Jobs Dependent on the EU* (February 2000) estimated 3,445,000 jobs.

12  NIESR.

13  NIESR.

14  NIESR.

15  The annual reports of the European Court of Auditors reveal that the share fell from 70.2 per cent in 1985 to 49.5 per cent in 1999.

16  Article 1 commits members to nothing more than 'the promotion of employment, improved living and working conditions, proper social protection, dialogue between management and labour, the development of human resources with a view to lasting high employment and the combating of exclusion'.

17  The original signatories of the Schengen Agreement – the Benelux, France and Germany – have since been joined by Austria, Denmark, Finland, Greece, Italy, Portugal, Spain and Sweden.

18  Although the EU made grants to help poor areas before 1989, the advent of Structural Funds that year transformed their impact. In the tranche for 1989–93 Britain received about £4 billion and for 1994–9 around £10 billion. The current allocations relate to 2000–6.

19  John Redwood – *Stars and Strife: The Coming Conflicts Between the USA and the European Union* (Palgrave, Basingstoke, 2001), p. 4.

20  Harold Macmillan – *Britain, the Commonwealth and Europe* (Conservative Political Centre, London, 1962).

21  Raymond Seitz – speech to Pilgrims' Dinner, 19 April 1994.

22  US International Trade Commission – *The Impact on the US Economy of Including the United Kingdom in a Free Trade Arrangement with the United States, Canada, and Mexico* (Publication 3339, August 2000).

23  Negotiations were initiated by Leon Brittan when he was the Competition then the Trade Commissioner, and his achievements are recorded in Leon Brittan – *A Diet of Brussels: The Changing Face of Europe* (Little Brown, London, 2000).

24  Margaret Thatcher – *Europe: The Future*, 24 June 1984.

25  NATO Berlin Communiqué, 3 June 1996.

26  Madeleine Albright – statement in Washington, 20 November 2000.

27  *Guardian*, 28 February 2001.

28  NATO Washington Declaration, 23 April 1999.

29  *Daily Telegraph*, 21 November 2000.

30  Jacques Chirac – speech to General Assembly of the North Atlantic Treaty Association in Strasbourg, 19 October 1999.

31  Macmillan.

32  Quoted in Uwe Kitzinger – *Diplomacy and Persuasion: How Britain Joined the Common Market* (Thames & Hudson, London, 1973), p. 184.

## Chapter 4

1  Gordon Brown, Hansard col 583–8, 27 October 1997.

2   *UK Membership of the Single Currency: An Assessment of
    the Five Economic Tests* (Treasury, London, 1997) sets the
    following questions:
    1.  *Cyclical Convergence* 'Are business cycles and
        economic structures compatible so that we and
        others could live comfortably with euro interest
        rates on a permanent basis?'
    2.  *Flexibility* 'If problems emerge is there sufficient
        flexibility to deal with them?'
    3.  *Investment* 'Would joining EMU create better
        conditions for firms making long-term decisions to
        invest in Britain?'
    4.  *Financial Services* 'What impact would entry into
        EMU have on the competitive position of the UK's
        financial services industry, particularly the City's
        wholesale markets?'
    5.  *Employment & Growth* 'In summary, will joining
        EMU promote higher growth, stability and a lasting
        increase in jobs?'
3   The whole tale is best told by Philip Stephens – *Politics
    and the Pound: The Conservatives' Struggle with Sterling*
    (Macmillan, London, 1996). Nigel Lawson – *The View
    from No 11: Memoirs of a Tory Radical* (Transworld,
    London, 1992) gives a brilliant exegesis of the
    economics of the ERM. Norman Lamont – *In Office*
    (Little Brown, London, 1999) offers a post hoc and self-
    serving assessment of its politics.
4   In an attempt to defend the krona from attack, the
    Swedish central bank raised interest rates to 500 per
    cent in September 1992 and still failed to fend off the
    speculators.
5   Michael Emerson et al. – *One Market, One Money: An*

*Evaluation of the Potential Benefits and Costs of Forming an Economic and Monetary Union* (OUP, Oxford, 1992).

6    Comprehensive economic arguments for joining are outlined in David Currie – *The Pros and Cons of EMU* (EIU, London, 1997), David Currie – *Will the Euro Work? The Ins and Outs of EMU* (EIU, London, 1998), Christopher Huhne – 'The Arguments For the Euro and European Monetary Union', in James Forder & Christopher Huhne – *Both Sides of the Coin* (Profile, London, 1999), Christopher Johnson – *In With the Euro Out With the Pound: The Single Currency for Britain* (Penguin, London, 1996) and Richard Layard et al. – *The Case for the Euro* (BiE, London, 2000).

7    Treasury Select Committee – *The World Economy and the Pre-Budget Report: Minutes of Evidence and Appendices* (TSO, London, January 1999), pp. 97–107.

8    The important measure is the share of traded goods, not the wider definition of current account receipts that adds in investment income and is often cited by opponents of the euro. It is easier to switch the geographic distribution of investments than goods, so they are less susceptible to the consequences of currency volatility. In any case, more than half our total trade in goods and services is with the EU.

9    Ministry of Agriculture, Fisheries & Food – *Agricultural Labour Input UK* (MAFF, London, 2001).

10   This all helps to explain why the National Farmers' Union has been strongly committed to British entry into the euro since it published its position paper *Economic and Monetary Union: An Agricultural Perspective* (NFU, London, 1995).

11   Textile and Clothing Strategy Group – *A National*

*Strategy for the UK Textile and Clothing Industry* (DTI, London, 2000), p. 34.

12 Memo from Andrew Fraser, chief executive of the Invest in Britain Bureau, to Stephen Byers, Trade and Industry Secretary, 7 May 2000. Quoted in *The Daily Telegraph*, 3 July 2000.

13 Memo from Stephen Gomersall, ambassador to Tokyo, to Colin Budd, Economic Director of the Foreign Office, 19 June 2000. Quoted in *The Times*, 4 July 2000.

14 *Financial Times*, 4 August 2000.

15 Ireland Industrial Development Agency – *Achieve European Competitive Advantage in Ireland* (IIDA, Dublin, 2000).

16 Ernst & Young – *European Investment Monitor: 1999 Results* (May 2000).

17 *BBC Breakfast with Frost*, 14 January 2001.

18 *Financial Times*, 6 February 2001.

19 *Financial Times*, 10 January 2001.

20 *Observer*, 27 May 2001.

21 *Financial Times*, 11 July 2000.

22 All the relevant companies are identified by Kitty Ussher in *Counting the Cost: 1999* (BiE, London, 2000) and *Counting the Cost: 2000* (BiE, London, 2001).

23 This rule of thumb is extrapolated from Cambridge Econometrics – *UK Job Dependence on Exports to the EU* (February 2000).

24 House of Commons Library – *Economic Policy & Statistics: The Cost of Unemployment*, 2 February 2001.

25 Bureau Européen des Unions de Consommateurs – *A Single Price for a Single Currency?*, December 1998.

26 Consumers' Association – *Cheaper Brands: More Choice, Lower Prices*, December 2000.

27  *Sunday Times*, 8 October 2000.

28  Jonquil Lowe – 'The Euro and the Consumer', pp. 104–9, in *Consumer Policy Review*, May–June 1998.

29  Fiona Earley – 'The UK Housing Market and EMU', in *Housing Finance Review*, 1998–9.

30  *Western Morning News*, 11 July 2000.

31  Andrew Rose & Eric van Wincoop – *National Money as a Barrier to International Trade: The Real Case for Currency Union* (California University, Berkeley, 2000). An even higher estimate is in Jeffrey Frankel & Andrew Rose – *An Estimate of the Effect of Common Currencies on Trade and Income* (California University, Berkeley, 2001).

32  Lehman Brothers – *Labour's Second Term: The Euro and Other Challenges* (June 2001).

33  Goldman Sachs – *UK Weekly Analyst*, 9 March 2001.

34  Some of the more cogent economic arguments against joining, from a variety of perspectives, can be found in Walter Eltis – *Britain, Europe and EMU* (Macmillan, London, 2000), James Forder – 'The Arguments Against the Euro and European Monetary Union', in James Forder & Christopher Huhne – *Both Sides of the Coin* (Profile, London, 1999), Geoff Martin – *Trade Unions, Public Services and the Euro* (TASC, London, 1999), John Mills – *Europe's Economic Dilemma* (Macmillan, London, 1998), John Redwood – *Our Currency, Our Country: The Dangers of European Monetary Union* (Penguin, London, 1997) and John Redwood – *Just Say No! 100 Arguments Against the Euro* (Politico's, London, 2001).

35  *Times*, 22 October 1988.

36  Norman Lamont – *Sovereign Britain* (Duckworth, London, 1995), pp. 42–3.

37  *Retailing Supermarketing*, 8 November 1996.

38   Chantrey Vellacott/Business for Sterling – *The Estimated
     Total One-Off Costs to the UK Private and Public Sectors,
     Should the UK Join the Euro* (BfS, London, 2000).

39   Trade and Industry Select Committee – *What Would the
     Euro Cost UK Business?: Report, together with the
     Proceedings of the Committee, Minutes of Evidence and
     Appendices* (TSO, London, November 2000), pp. 57–60.

40   For example this is the view of the German Institute
     for Small and Medium-Sized Business Research.

41   *CBI Europe Brief,* December 1996.

42   Bannock Consulting – *An Estimate of the One-Off
     Transition Costs to the UK of Joining the Euro* (July 2001).

43   *Sunday Times,* 17 June 2001.

44   *CBI Europe Brief.*

45   John Nott – *Britain and the Pound: A Prosperous Future for
     Britain* (Conservative Central Office, London, 1999), p. 13.

46   Julian Morris – *E-future or €-past?: How the Internet is
     Leaving the Euro Behind* (BfS, London, 2000).

47   *BBC Newsnight,* 15 June 2000.

48   Nott, p. 22.

49   European Commission – *Draft Tax Policy in the European
     Union: Priorities for the Years Ahead,* 23 May 2001.

50   European Central Bank – *Annual Report: 1999* (ECB,
     Frankfurt, 1999), p. 2.

51   Recent examples include International Monetary Fund
     – *United Kingdom: Staff Report for the 1999 Article IV
     Consultation* (March 2000), Organisation for Economic
     Co-operation and Development – *Economic Survey of the
     United Kingdom 2000* (June 2000), Treasury Select
     Committee – *Economic and Monetary Union: Report and
     Proceedings of the Committee* (July 2000), ABN-AMRO
     Bank – *Euroland Economics Update: Should the UK Join*

*EMU?* (August 2000), GrahamBishop.com – *Britain and*
*€uroland: 4Q 2000* (January 2001), Pricewaterhouse-
Coopers – *EMU Convergence Index* (January 2001), Ernst
& Young ITEM Club – *The UK and EMU: Ships Passing*
*in the Night?* (March 2001) and Lehman Brothers –
*Labour's Second Term: The Euro and Other Challenges*
(June 2001).
52  Robert Mundell – 'A theory of optimum currency
    areas', in *American Economic Review*, vol 51, 1961.

## Chapter 5

1  Winston Churchill – speech in The Hague, 7 May
   1948.
2  Legal and Constitutional Implications of United
   Kingdom Membership of the European Communities
   (Cmnd 3301, HMSO White Paper, May 1967).
3  Enoch Powell – speech to Conservative Party
   Conference, 13 October 1971.
4  Tony Benn, Hansard col 1751–64, 27 October 1971.
5  Article 5 of the NATO Treaty states that 'the Parties
   agree that an armed attack against one or more of
   them in Europe or North America shall be
   considered an attack against them all and
   consequently they agree that, if such an armed attack
   occurs, each of them, in exercise of the right of
   individual or collective self-defence recognised by
   Article 51 of the Charter of the United Nations, will
   assist the Party or Parties so attacked by taking
   forthwith, individually and in concert with the other
   Parties, such action as it deems necessary, including

the use of armed force, to restore and maintain the security of the North Atlantic area'.

6   A perfect example of the unconvincing intellectual somersaults that anti-Europeans perform in order to attack the idea of pooled sovereignty while not openly arguing for withdrawal from Europe is Noel Malcolm – 'Sense on Sovereignty', in Martin Holmes (ed) – *The Eurosceptical Reader* (Macmillan, London, 1996).

7   One of the best expositions of the case for pooled sovereignty, from which the rope analogy is drawn, is Geoffrey Howe – speech to London School of Economics, 8 June 1990; another is George Schultz – speech to National Academy of Engineering, 4 October 1989.

8   Harold Macmillan – *Britain, the Commonwealth and Europe* (Conservative Political Centre, London, 1962).

9   The United Kingdom and the European Communities (Cmnd 4715, HMSO White Paper, July 1971).

10   Margaret Thatcher – speech in Hendon, 19 May 1975.

11   Romano Prodi – speech to CBI conference, 6 November 2000.

12   Joint letter from Jacques Chirac, French President, and Helmut Kohl, German Chancellor, to Tony Blair, President of the European Council, 5 June 1998.

13   Jacques Chirac – speech to Bundestag, 27 June 2000.

14   Joschka Fischer – speech to German–British 2000 award ceremony, 24 January 2001.

15   Bigger examples include the Latin Monetary Union formed in 1865 by Belgium, France, Greece, Italy and Switzerland, and the Scandinavian Monetary Union formed in 1872 by Denmark, Norway and Sweden.

16   Bernard Connolly – *The Rotten Heart of Europe: The*

*Dirty War for Europe's Money* (Faber & Faber, London, 1995), p. 10.

17 French PS – The Socialist European Project: Draft Proposal, 14 May 2001; German SPD – Responsibility for Europe: Draft Proposal, 30 April 2001.

18 This argument is brilliantly expounded in Alan Milward – *The European Rescue of the Nation-State* (Routledge, London, 1992).

19 Winston Churchill – speech to University of Zurich, 19 September 1946.

20 Ernest Bevin, Hansard col 383–409, 22 January 1948.

21 Quoted in Hugo Young – *This Blessed Plot: Britain and Europe from Churchill to Blair* (Macmillan, London, 1998), p. 118.

22 Membership of the European Communities (Cmnd 3269, HMSO White Paper, May 1967).

23 Britain and the European Communities: An Economic Assessment (Cmnd 4289, HMSO White Paper, February 1970).

24 Con O'Neill – *Britain's Entry into the European Community: Report on the Negotiations of 1970–72* (Frank Cass, London, 2000), p. 40.

25 John Major – speech in Ellesmere Port, 31 May 1994.

26 John Major – speech in Leiden, 7 September 1994.

27 The original Six signatories to the Treaty of Rome – Belgium, France, Germany, Italy, Luxembourg and the Netherlands – were enlarged to Nine in 1973 when Britain, Denmark and Ireland joined. The number rose to ten with Greece in 1981, to twelve with Portugal and Spain in 1986 and to fifteen with Austria, Finland and Sweden in 1995.

28 The dates of outstanding applications are:

| Turkey | 14 April 1987 |
| Cyprus | 3 July 1990 |
| Malta | 16 July 1990 (frozen in 1996, reactivated in 1998) |
| Hungary | 31 March 1994 |
| Poland | 5 April 1994 |
| Romania | 22 June 1995 |
| Slovakia | 27 June 1995 |
| Latvia | 13 October 1995 |
| Estonia | 24 November 1995 |
| Lithuania | 8 December 1995 |
| Bulgaria | 14 December 1995 |
| Czech Republic | 17 January 1996 |
| Slovenia | 10 June 1996 |

29  It was decided in 1999 to recognise Turkey as a candidate and to help it prepare for accession, although negotiations will begin only when it achieves the necessary political criteria.

30  Larry Siedentop – *Democracy in Europe* (Allen Lane, London, 2000).

31  The most important statements of the opening gambits of Britain, France and Germany prior to the negotiations at the 2004 IGC are Tony Blair – speech to Polish Stock Exchange, 6 October 2000; Jacques Chirac – speech to Bundestag, 27 June 2000; Lionel Jospin – speech to Foreign Press Association, 28 May 2001; French PS – The Socialist European Project: Draft Proposal, 14 May 2001; Joschka Fischer – speech to Humboldt University, 12 May 2000; and German SPD – Responsibility for Europe: Draft Proposal, 30 April 2001.

32  For accessible summaries of the workings of the institutions, see Timothy Bainbridge – *The Penguin*

*Companion to European Union* (Penguin, London, 2000) and John Pinder – *The Building of the European Union* (OUP, Oxford, 1998).

33   The European Court of Justice in Luxembourg should not be confused with the European Court of Human Rights in Strasbourg, which is an organ of the Council of Europe.

34   In fact there are only two countries less vigilant than Britain. The members have set themselves the target of implementing a minimum of 98.5 per cent of all internal market directives, and every six months the European Commission releases a 'Single Market Scoreboard' to identify how they are performing. The recent figures are:

| Member | May 2001 | Nov 2000 |
|---|---|---|
| Sweden | 99.5% | 98.8% |
| Denmark | 98.8% | 98.9% |
| Finland | 98.6% | 98.7% |
| Spain | 98.2% | 98.4% |
| Luxembourg | 98.0% | 96.8% |
| The Netherlands | 98.0% | 97.5% |
| Belgium | 97.6% | 97.1% |
| Italy | 97.4% | 96.8% |
| Portugal | 97.3% | 95.6% |
| Germany | 97.2% | 96.9% |
| Austria | 96.8% | 97.1% |
| Ireland | 96.7% | 96.4% |
| United Kingdom | 96.7% | 97.3% |
| France | 96.5% | 95.5% |
| Greece | 95.2% | 93.5% |

35   The fall and rise of British economic strength is well told in Geoffrey Owen – *From Empire to Europe: The*

*Decline and Revival of British Industry Since the Second World War* (HarperCollins, London, 1999).

36  Many commentators argue that higher investment not greater liberalisation is the real key to European competitiveness. For a business perspective see Adair Turner – *Just Capital: The Liberal Economy* (Macmillan, London, 2001); for a more traditional Rhinelander or stakeholder approach see Will Hutton – *The State We're In* (Jonathan Cape, London, 1995).

37  According to the Organisation for Economic Co-operation and Development, the figures for GDP per head in 1999 are:

| *Member* | *Sterling equivalent* |
| --- | --- |
| Luxembourg | £24,300 |
| Denmark | £16,300 |
| Ireland | £15,600 |
| The Netherlands | £15,500 |
| Austria | £15,200 |
| Belgium | £15,000 |
| Germany | £14,600 |
| Sweden | £14,200 |
| Finland | £14,100 |
| United Kingdom | £13,800 |
| France | £13,500 |
| Italy | £13,500 |
| Spain | £11,200 |
| Portugal | £10,200 |
| Greece | £9,100 |

38  According to the European Commission, the figures for productivity per worker in 2000 are:

| Member | Index of productivity per hour worked (where 100 is the EU average) |
|---|---|
| Luxembourg | 194.6 |
| Belgium | 124.8 |
| The Netherlands | 118.8 |
| Italy | 112.7 |
| France | 111.1 |
| Denmark | 109.7 |
| Ireland | 105.0 |
| Austria | 103.9 |
| Germany | 103.1 |
| Finland | 95.7 |
| Sweden | 93.2 |
| United Kingdom | 92.4 |
| Spain | 80.0 |
| Greece | 67.2 |
| Portugal | 62.4 |

39 Presidency Conclusions, Lisbon European Council, 23–24 March 2000.

40 Almost half of Danish exports go to the euro-zone but they are not subject to currency volatility because the krone has been pegged to the euro from the start. Furthermore, Denmark receives virtually no inward investment (just 2.5 per cent of the EU total in 1999) and the krone is not a major trading currency (accounting for only 0.2 per cent of the daily turnover in the foreign exchanges).

41 *Daily Telegraph*, 24 November 1997.

42 Margaret Thatcher – speech to Conservative Group for Europe, 16 April 1975.

43 Tony Blair – speech to launch of 'Britain in Europe', 14 October 1999.